# Behaviour Management
# with Young Children

What a privilege to read a book written by the person that has had the most impact on my classroom teaching and the whole ethos of our school. *Behaviour Management with Young Children* brings together Bill's insight into behaviour management and Elizabeth's understanding of young children and has resulted in a practical and realistic behaviour management manual that will be easily accessible to teachers in the early years… I shall be recommending it to all my teaching and support staff as essential reading.

*Debbie Hoy, Headteacher, Brookland Infant & Nursery School, Cheshunt, Hertfordshire*

As headteacher of an infant and nursery school with children from 3–7 years old, Bill and Elizabeth's book is what we have been waiting for. A comprehensive guide to the effective behaviour management of our youngest children, it will be essential reading for all our staff… This is a book which can easily be read from cover to cover, as it is difficult to put down, but for busy practitioners it is equally useful to dip into if you want help with a specific aspect of behaviour management. [The] approaches are firmly based on sound theory and what works with children, and Elizabeth clearly describes the practical and effective application of those ideas in the earliest years of education. The book is a delight to read and will be a constant source of inspiration and guidance to us all.

*Cathy Whalen, Headteacher, Mousehold Infant and Nursery School, Norwich, Norfolk*

… With their feet firmly planted in the reality of the classroom Bill and Elizabeth show how subtle changes to everyday interchanges between adults and pupils can have an enormous impact upon pupil success. It is amazing how simple yet effective the strategies outlined here are. The ideas and concepts shared in the book are accessible to all staff and we can all recognise some of ourselves and our pupils in Bill's delightful illustrations. This book will make a difference not only to the behaviour of pupils but also to the sanity of teachers. It is a must for every staff room!

*Jane Bellamy, Headteacher, Wold Newton School, Wold Newton, Driffield, East Riding of Yorkshire*

# BEHAVIOUR MANAGEMENT WITH YOUNG CHILDREN

## Crucial First Steps with Children 3–7 Years

## Bill Rogers and Elizabeth McPherson

Los Angeles • London • New Delhi • Singapore

First published 2008

SAGE Publications Ltd
1 Oliver's Yard
55 City Road
London EC1Y 1SP

SAGE Publications Inc.
2455 Teller Road
Thousand Oaks, California 91320

SAGE Publications India Pvt Ltd
B 1/I 1 Mohan Cooperative Industrial Area
Mathura Road
New Delhi 110 044

SAGE Publications Asia-Pacific Pte Ltd
33 Pekin Street #02-01
Far East Square
Singapore 048763

**Library of Congress Control Number: 2007939519**

British Library Cataloguing in Publication data

A catalogue record for this book is available from the British
Library

**ISBN 978-1-84787-363-7**
**ISBN 978-1-84787-364-4 (pbk)**

Typeset by Dorwyn, Wells, Somerset
Printed in Great Britain by Cromwell Press, Trowbridge,
Wiltshire
Printed on paper from sustainable resources

# Contents

*Note*:

The text shifts from first person to second person (pronoun) in both case example and general writing. We believe this best enables each author's writing – without (on each occasion) having to identify the writer/speaker.

Often the teacher in the case studies is female; no sexist emphasis here, just common reality at early years level. When I am teaching in an early years class, as a male, I am often a 'transitory novelty' (until they get used to me – Bill).

The percentage of distracting and disruptive children – the behaviourally challenging and children with diagnosed behaviour disorders – are male (from our experience). Again no sexist emphasis – just reality. On an 80/20 per cent split, disruptive and challenging behaviours are nominated as male. (See also Morgan and Jenson, 1988; Rogers, 2003a.)

# Acknowledgements

Elizabeth and I want to thank the many children we have taught over the years; some of whom feature prominently in this book. We have changed their names (for ethical reasons). No doubt they would be surprised to find their stories addressed here; their stories have become part of our teaching history. This is the nature of our profession – 'our' children are more than children in a class. Early years teachers care for 'their' children in a very protective way. We are often thinking of them well outside the school day. Hopefully that is true of any caring teacher, but at this age (early years) our concern for the children's emotional well-being and psychological safety is paramount. We also 'rack our brains' as to how we can best enable, encourage, support and maintain a positive learning environment for them.

We also want to thank our colleagues; our fellow teachers. The days are long gone when teachers worked in professional isolation; colleague support is crucial to our profession. We thank our colleagues for what they have taught us and for the moral – and professional – support we have enjoyed in our respective teaching journeys.

We particularly want to thank our typist – Felicia. Hand-writing is so old-fashioned today but my contribution (Bill) was reams of A4 'Biroed' and patiently interpreted by Felicia Schmidt. Elizabeth's contribution was always neatly word-processed.

Lastly we want to thank our publisher, Sage Publications (London), for all their support. From the outset Marianne Lagrange (senior editor) and the team: Jude Bowen; Matthew Waters; Jennifer Crisp; Vanessa Harwood and Imogen Roome.

*Bill Rogers and Elizabeth McPherson*
*Melbourne, October, 2007*

# Preface

## How this book came about

Elizabeth and I have both taught at early years level (pp. 109f) and are acutely aware of the demands of teaching children at this age level (4–7 years) – particularly reception age. We are aware of the special sensibilities, anxieties and social sense that 4- and 5-year-olds bring to a class of 25 others (in that unique, new, setting called 'school').

Children will spend a third of their waking day in this place. There are specific and necessary demands made on their cognitive and social-relational understanding. There is a wide variance of preparedness and home backgrounds that we – as teachers – have no control over that will assist or hinder those demands. As an individual teacher – as a school community – we cannot compensate for a child's home background; we can build a positive, and safe, learning community.

It is essential to establish, day one, a psychologically safe environment that can enable (even enthuse) their learning, and workable – and positive – social relationships.

We have paid special attention to the 'establishment phase' of the year. We are aware of both the psychological and developmental *readiness* children bring to those first days and weeks of their school life. And it is during this time – crucially – that we need to establish ourselves as teacher-leaders with confidence and respect.

We will, during this time, need to teach (and reinforce) what is appropriate and inappropriate behaviour, and we will need to discipline children; to correct behaviour; to apply behaviour consequences. It is an essential aspect of our teacher leadership. We also need to encourage our children[1] to build confidence, to engage and enthuse our children; this is essential and primary – *but we do have to discipline*; that is what this book is about. How do we enable that balance, in our behaviour leadership, between building a safe, positive learning environment alongside necessary discipline?[2]

We are particularly concerned about the nature and use of our *characteristic* language (as teacher-leaders) when we discipline children, whether it is 'merely' calling-out behaviour; inappropriate loudness – through to pushing and shoving and bullying.

What we say when we speak to a child about poor, or inappropriate, or un-acceptable behaviour, is essential. Simply telling children what not to do ("Don't call out ...", "Don't talk while I'm teaching.", "Don't push ...", etc.) is of little help *as discipline*. It is simply telling them what we *do not* want them to do rather than what we *do* want them to do. There is a time to use a 'don't' message but it is probably the most overused word in discipline along with the interrogative – "Why". "*Why* are you calling out?", "*Why* haven't you started work ...?", "You're not supposed to be out of your seat now *are you?*" (p 50).

We are aware that the conscious use of our language (in behaviour management *and* encouragement contexts) has a significant effect on the degree, and kind, of understanding children have about their behaviour.

We are also acutely aware that at this age (particularly for 4 and 5-year-olds) there are children who are not easily aware that what they are doing is 'wrong', e.g. when they call out, butt in on others, elbow and push, snatch and grab, use put-downs, tease, swear ...

Engaging a child's behaviour awareness and co-operation is no mean feat. We have sought to identify those behaviour management and discipline practices that take note of the child's moral and psychological development and seek to engage their understanding and co-operation.[3]

We believe that positive behaviour management and discipline is not based merely on teacher personality (important as that is); it is also based on conscious skill.

There are many case studies (from our classes) that inform the practices and skills we have found helpful and practical, and (more importantly) enable us to keep the focus on a safe – respectful – relationship between teacher and child(ren).

We have reflected long, and hard, on our teaching experience. A significant part of my teaching experience has involved mentoring or team-teaching with a particular focus on peer-coaching (Bill). We can go for years, in our profession, without having a colleague whom we trust come into our class(es) and work alongside us and (later) over a tea or coffee, discuss and initiate professional self-reflection. We can then use that reflection to further reflect on the utility, value and effect of our *characteristic* behaviour leadership.

It is in that sense, in writing this book, we have sought to encourage *professional self-reflection.* We have also paid special attention to the crucial subject of colleague support. Teaching can be a somewhat 'lonely' profession in some schools (working with 'minors' all day). Colleague support is important and necessary in meeting the moral and professional needs of individual teachers. Nowhere is this more acute than when we seek to work with children who are behaviourally challenging or who have been diagnosed as having behaviour disorders (Chapter 6).

We want to thank the many classes, the individual children and colleagues we have taught (and worked with) over the years. This book is – in part – their story as well as ours. We have learned so much from the children we have taught – we have learned about ourselves (our frustrations, fallibility and our successes); we have also learned practices and skills we pass on here.

We believe we have done what we went into teaching for – to make a difference in the lives of the children we have worked with.

# Introduction

## Bill: 'Scuttling down the corridors of memory'[4]

When I first began primary teaching (30 years ago now) they mostly gave me the older children (ages 9–11). As a male teacher I was expected to be more effective at 'discipline with the boys'. Also I would 'naturally' teach football, cricket, swimming, volleyball and dance! (I had never played Australian Rules football; I grew up in England as a child.) Part of my first year involved SART teaching (Special Assistance Resource Teaching); I took classes across the school to give 'release time' to grade teachers. I designed a range of activities (art, drama, music, story-telling ...). I wanted this SART time to be more than 'fill-in' time; I wanted to enthuse, inform, engage and (even) educate. It was during this time that I began to understand the management (and discipline) of early years classes in any meaningful way. It was a new experience.

With my trusty guitar (bought during army service years before) I taught such songs as 'London Bridge Is Falling Down', 'The Wheels On the Bus ...', 'Alice's Restaurant' (one of Arlo Guthrie's songs ... I'd change Alice to children's names; they loved that) and also 'Miss Polly Had a Dolly ...'. When I got to the part about 'the doctor came with his bag and his hat ...' I changed it to ' the doctor came with *her* coat and *her* hat ...'.

When I changed the gender many boys *and* girls would raise their hand (or call out) "Women can't be doctors!" It was staggering, back there in the 1970s, to see such mindsets. I would, of course, stop the song and 're-educate'. "Women can be anything (except fathers) ...", and then *after* the song discuss why, and how, women can be 'anything'. It is hard to believe now.

Gender inclusion has (thankfully) come a long way. It was – however – still somewhat of a novelty to have a male teacher teaching 4- and 5-year-olds back then. I have lost count of the times when children (even 11-year-old children) have called me 'mum'; unconsciously. I take it as kind of a compliment and change the register of my voice (to a higher pitch) to make the pretended point. Five-year-olds do have a sense of humour!

I was acutely conscious of my 'maleness' when working with young children. I was consciously aware of size, voice register and presence (always getting down to their eye level – a bit harder on the knees now, at 60!). I was also acutely aware of how I 'came across' in any discipline contexts. We still had corporal punishment in those days and like many younger teachers I strongly disagreed with *any* corporal punishment.[5]

In time I also took on the role of art teacher (in a large suburban primary school) though I am badly colour blind and was not art trained (naturally; that is why I was given the art room). I thoroughly enjoyed it. I had 5-year-olds earnestly trying to teach me 'my colours'. One young lad even made up a colour chart for me with the names of the colours, "so you can learn them properly Mr Rogers!"

Later I took on 5–6-year-olds for a year, my first 'real' class. As a subject teacher (art, music, library, Languages other than English (LOTE)) older children often perceive the subject teacher as less 'real' (that is, important; 'central' to their school life) than their *class* teacher. I had some 7-year-olds say to me, "When will you be a 'real' teacher Mr Rogers?" They meant 'When will you have a *class*?' Those years tested me; many of the lessons I learned about establishing a class in those crucial first days and weeks; the fundamental nature of routines, as well as stated rules; the need for clear, respectful, appropriately firm, corrective language balanced by thoughtful encouragement, was learned in those years and has stayed with me in my teaching journey.

## The privilege of teaching (Elizabeth)

I would like to point out that I am in no way, shape or form an 'expert'. I am, however, someone who has sought to do her best, who has made mistakes and learnt from them. I am someone who I believe has some helpful ideas that have worked for me and will – hopefully – be of some benefit to others. Above all I am a parent, and that has made me reflect most of all on children, parents, carers and teachers (and the important relationships between us).

I thought I loved and protected the children in my care (even got 'my back up' if other staff members said something negative about 'my' children) but now I know that those feelings are amplified a thousand fold with one's own children. Sending your child off to school is scary, and for some, heart-wrenching (p. 135). We as teachers are entrusted with the care of little ones who – to their parents and carers – are their entire world and their reason for living. Teaching is a privilege and one of the most important jobs on the planet. If life as we know it ceased to exist and we had to start again who would be of true value ... pop stars and actors? No ... it would be farmers, doctors, builders and *teachers* (food, health, shelter, knowledge and the learning skills).

# The establishment phase of the year

## Our leadership

There has been much research devoted to this essential phase in the life of a class group – as well as how successfully an individual child integrates into 'the group'. Children have a natural readiness – a developmental and psychological readiness – formed (in part) from earlier experiences at playgroups and at kindergarten; or group experiences such as dance/music ... They bring that 'readiness' with them to their first classes at school.

When most children come into a school they expect the adults, their teachers, to 'lead' them. They have – already – experienced a range of adult leaders (including parents, carers, grandcarers, other care-givers or 'teachers'). They 'know' (emotively) how some adults 'don't mean what they say'; how some adults are unclear, uncertain, 'not confident' in what they say, and expect, of children. They do not use this language of course, but they know when a teacher is 'in charge'. They also know when the teacher 'knows what they are doing' as they lead groups and individuals. They know, too, they do not like 'bossy', mean, petty, petulant, churlish teachers. Even if they comply with authoritarian 'styles' of leadership (not all children will) it will not mean the children under such leadership are actually co-operative, or learning what is planned within the overall curriculum.

As teachers, we 'earn' our leadership by the extent to which we are able to convey confidence in what we are doing *when we lead*:

- The kind of language we use to 'calm', 'settle' and focus a class (p. 11–15) every day of our teaching life.
- Rules/routines/procedural norms and explanations that have been thoughtfully communicated over that critical first week (p. 12–13).
- Our ability to convey a sense of control by the teacher; control *of the events of classroom life*. We distinguish between 'controlling a child' and *controlling situations and contexts* within which we lead, guide, discipline and encourage our children. This is derived from *careful planning* of routines; clear (and fair) rules; classroom organisation (seating arrangements/work stations, etc.) and teaching and learning arrangements.

- The kind of discipline (from corrective language to behaviour consequences) that we utilise daily. Confident discipline that is communicated calmly, positively and – where necessary – with firm assertion.
- The balance between necessary correction (and consequences) and necessary encouragement.
- And, of course, by our ability to engage – and enthuse – in the teaching and learning journey.

# Discipline

## The language of correction

Whether it is repeated calling out; chatting while the teacher is talking; poking, pushing, 'fiddling' – on the mat; squabbling; reactive behaviour; whining, moaning and whingeing – or whether it is more serious behaviours such as dangerous play, using equipment dangerously; out-of-control tantrums or bullying; effective teachers will need to *plan* for corrective language within their overall behaviour leadership. It still concerns me that many teachers (particularly beginning teachers) plan assiduously for a unit of work (or even an individual lesson) but do not actually *plan* for how they ought to address typical distracting and disruptive behaviours or the more serious behaviour concerns. This is also true for children with behaviour disorders who need particular – individual – behaviour plans that are as acutely developed as any individual lesson plan (see Chapter 6).

Discipline is primarily concerned with enabling children to be *aware* of and *own* their behaviour. Children need to know, and understand, that some behaviours are not merely unhelpful or inconsiderate; they are also wrong. Discipline is never (or should never be) merely an end in itself – the means *and* ends of discipline are to enable children' awareness about their behaviour and responsibility to others.

Good rules (planned, fair and clear) also highlight an individual's responsibility. Discipline is often seen primarily as punishment; the *consequential side of discipline* is essential but only within the aims of discipline noted above. A good consequence (in this sense) also considers *what* the child is learning about their responsibility within relational justice and accountability (see Chapter 5). While there are obviously degrees of seriousness regarding child behaviour in class (and non-class settings) children will need discipline for their own and others' welfare.

Good discipline has several functions.[6]

1. *It provides a safe, relational, context*. When a teacher outlines what behaviours are right and fair (and why), she enables, assures and teaches responsible co-

operative behaviour. A good teacher will do this by explanation *and* discussion. Any subsequent discipline will, then, have a reference to what the class group has discussed. It is also essential that responsible behaviour is *taught*, acknowledged, affirmed and encouraged.

2. Discipline *teaches* behaviour. Good discipline has an educational function when correction takes place (hopefully more by thoughtful 'design' than by default!). When a teacher disciplines with dignity, whether 'minor' corrective reminders (such as when we address calling out, or talking while the teacher is talking ...) or more serious behaviours, the teacher is, in effect, also teaching what is fair and reasonable as well as what is right and wrong.[7] Even basic reminders about manners such as 'please', 'thanks', 'can I borrow ...', 'excuse me' (when moving into, or past, personal space ...) all teach basic fairness and consideration. Good discipline also teaches all children that there *need* to be fair rules (based on rights) and corresponding responsibilities (p. 44–6).

3. Good discipline is also *preventative*. When we establish fair rules *and* routines; when we use *positive* corrective language; when we set up appropriate and fair consequences, we prevent the likelihood of repeated distracting and disruptive behaviour.

4. Discipline also *protects*. When a teacher disciplines a student who is teasing, pushing, shoving, grabbing or hurting others, she is protecting the rights of those whose learning is distracted or disrupted; they are protecting the rights of the aggrieved, the maligned, the bullied, the hurt ...

Thoughtful rules and routines, established (and maintained) in an age-related way, minimise disruption. They do not eliminate distraction and disruption but they do provide a known framework that can minimise and (in that sense) prevent undue distraction and disruption.

Children thrive on sensible and fair routines and boundaries ... knowing what to expect from their teachers and knowing that these rules, routines and boundaries are not merely adult impositions; they are for the good of all.

I once had a class of children lined up for a library lesson. We all stood lined up outside chatting quietly. I was answering question after question from the children and just having a nice time interacting with them. A 'parent helper' said, "I don't know how you do it!", referring to 'keeping them lined up, quiet, happy, keeping several conversations on the go ...' I had never thought of it as anything unusual, it is simply that children know the rules at school and they operate (most of the time) within those guidelines. Our children do this when we convey confident and positive expectation *and* encouragement.

Organisation
I believe it is essential to keep the classroom tidy (pp. 20–1, 30). Label things

with words (and pictures); have a place for everything and everything in its place. Bookshelves, reading corner (couches and pillows, if you are lucky) sports equipment tub, named tubs (for their ongoing classwork) and bag hooks, lost property box, spare paper tub ... the list goes on. There are lots of people and personalities coexisting in a small space for the majority of the day and the week. Not everyone is going to be in a good mood every day, and keeping things organised and physically comfortable keeps things running as smoothly as possible. When tempers are frayed, children are tired and you 'have had enough', it helps the situation if chairs are not so close they are tripping each other up or bags are not strewn across walkways (p. 20). Make sure your children know where to find things by talking (and walking) them through the places and spaces that make up 'our classroom' in the establishment phase of the year.

5. Good discipline enables a sense of justice. When children see their teacher manage child behaviour with appropriate – and fair – correction *and* consequences, they are assured of a just learning environment *for all children.*

## The bad-day syndrome

Before we say very much more in this text we want to stress that it is one thing to say what we believe 'ought' to be good practice in discipline and behaviour management and what is the emotive reality – day after day after day ...

I was teaching a class of 5–6-year-olds and a lad persistently poked at, and annoyed, a couple of other boys while I was seeking to teach the class. During this whole-class teaching time the lad *seemed* to be doing all he could to gain attention from peers and teachers alike. (I was team-teaching.) I directed him several times to 'keep his hands and feet safe' and face the front 'with eyes and ears'. Each time he sulked in response to my direction and made an attentionally postural gesture of 'forced compliance'.

My colleague looked anxiously across at me; she seemed to be saying, "Tell me it's not just me ... now you can see what I have to put up with ... Day after day after day ...".

I continued with the whole-class teaching. The lad got up and started walking around at the back of the classroom. Naturally there was some giggling and 'watching' by most of the rest of the class. Some children looked at me (as the 'new' teacher) a little concerned; apprehensive about what I would do as the 'other' teacher.

I directed Karl back to the mat. Already in my mind I was considering how I might need to use some in-class time-out measure. He stomped back to his place on the mat, but in a different spot.

I was consciously aware (for the fifteen-thousandth time in my teaching life!) of the daily challenge of how to balance the ongoing welfare and rights of the group with the behaviour of one or two individuals.

We got through 'the lesson' with several residual grunts and annoyingly inappropriate laughter from Karl. During on-task learning time he was frequently off-task and tried, on a few occasions, to wander off – away from his table group. My colleague came over to me at one point, and said, with some weariness, "He's like that all the time". It certainly seemed so (in this, my first lesson with this class).

Later my colleague and I developed an individual behaviour plan with Karl (one-to-one in non-contact time, away from his class peers).[8]

Even though this lad had been diagnosed with 'autistic spectrum disorder' (Asperger's syndrome) I believed it was important not to simply give him 'too much rope'; to treat him *so* differently as to effectively excuse his behaviour *because* of his autism. In effect I did not want my colleague and I to treat him as 'a victim' of his disorder.

It was not easy. It never is. There was improvement in response to the individual behaviour plan. Each lesson, though, had that range of frustrating incidents; often 'small', though there was clearly improvement overall with the class and Karl. Colleague support was crucial, and valued.

There are days when 'the one or two main offenders' are absent and at roll call there is almost a collective sigh of relief from the other children. It is unfortunate that we sometimes feel relieved when the most difficult children are away as they are often the ones in greatest need of the safe and consistent environment that school can provide.

Whatever strategy, skill, approach we share with you in this text we are more than aware of the bad-day syndrome. That feeling – naturally stressful in those many emotional moments – when we are called to exercise corrective management in the midst of a busy lesson. The frustration, the annoyance, the need to frequently 'think ahead' and our concern about the 80–90 per cent of children affected by the disruptive behaviour of a few.

There will be days when we 'snap' – we will say the inappropriate thing; we will get angry on 'small issues' (because of the build-up of frustration); we will react in ways we did not mean to (hopefully!). There will be days when frustration, tiredness, even jadedness affect our behaviour as a teacher-leader. This is normal; human. We are eminently fallible.

What we are talking about here, in this book, is what we do as teacher-leaders on *most* days and what we ought to do *characteristically*. These practices and skills are based on what we believe, and value about human dignity as it interacts with the need to discipline.

The caveat is there however; *bad-day notwithstanding.*

# Chapter 1

## The critical first days and first week

### Day one – first meeting

There are 20 – or more – children sitting on the carpet the first year of primary school in front of you. It is your first day with your class. (Reception – 4- and 5-year-olds.) The children are – naturally – excited. Some are anxious; a few confused; some are just 'being themselves' (annoyingly). There is a lot of natural, normal, kinaesthetic energy here. Some of these children have been to playschool and kindergarten; some have loving and thoughtful and caring parents and carers; some have tired, frustrated parents and carers and are subject to inconsistent parenting and discipline. Some of these children have witnessed disturbing things – already – in their young lives; and not just on television.

They will need reassurance, guidance and direction – *from the outset*. From these first moments they will need to be taught – and encouraged – in those behaviours that will enable social co-operation and focused learning.

They will get used to 'sitting on the mat' – that carpet area facing their teacher. They will get used to putting their hands up to share or ask questions; to take their turn; to wait … think (perhaps) before they speak; to co-operate with their peers … That is all to come. Now they face their teacher; day one. They face the significant adult they will be with for most of each day, five days a week, throughout the school year.

They sit there, some cross-legged and (already) attentive, others are quite restless. We have to initiate *and sustain* whole-class attention: a key skill that will become second nature to us and – hopefully – reciprocated in our children.

Prior to this first day the children will – fortunately – have had:

- Transition days, easing children into the new world of 'school'.
- Some schools will start with half days, others with (say) Wednesdays off.
- Some with 'reception only play times' gradually overlapping with 'buddies play times' until they go to full play times with the rest of the school (see pp. 35, 36).
- Transition is vital to easing children into school in a positive way.
- Having tables set out with play activities (similar to a kindergarten set-up) is a useful way to get the children settled for the first week or so (depending on the dynamics of your class) and letting them play until the clingy, tearful parents and carers have left is very useful and allows you to deal with the more difficult cases (p. 134f).
- Parents/carers have had information packs and literature (that they have hopefully read) about how to assist their child's transition to school (p. 137). Activities such as labelling their uniform and letting them try it on, explaining what happens at school, role-playing, trying out the play equipment are all important activities that enable this significant transition in their lives.

# Play

It is crucial, in the early stages of the year, to allow time for play. Children have come from kindergarten (which is almost exclusively play) into a more formal structured primary school environment. To go from a 'play-rich' environment, into an environment that requires you to be 'on-task' at a desk, would, I am sure you will agree, be a shock to the system.

At the beginning of the year, I would set the tables up with various activities, puzzles on one table, drawing materials on another, a bucket of mobiles on the floor, etc. Children were then able to enter the classroom and begin their day in a familiar, non-threatening way, and as lingering parents and carers eventually departed, we were able to pack away and begin some whole-class, focused learning time on the mat. As the initial transition weeks progressed we were able to shift gradually to the more formal routine … bags on hooks, take-home books in the tub, straight on the mat for roll call. Incorporating moments of play into the rigours of the day can enable children to relax and celebrate their achievements. Using play in learning activities is also a positive way to enforce concepts that you are teaching. Be it hands-on play using different-sized containers with water or grain to demonstrate volume and capacity, cooking activities and puppet plays to demonstrate different writing genres, or memory games to teach sight words, play can be weaved into almost anything and can help to develop a love of learning.

That is not to say that play only has a role at transition time. It can also be used as a vehicle for learning (social interaction, motor skills, role playing, spatial relations, the list goes on) as well as a 'reward' celebration. I used to allocate Friday afternoons as 'developmental play time'. I would arrange various play activities ranging from collage and paper jewellery making to baby dolls and cars. I would use a task management board (similar to that used for literacy groups) and ask children to put their names next to the play activities set up for that afternoon. This enabled the children to try new games and activities, learn new skills and make new friends. I would then use this time to make annotated assessments of what the children were playing and learning through that play time. Without trying to sound too 'academic' about the whole thing ... Friday afternoons, end of the week, tired little kids, a bit of play is good for them. (Elizabeth)[9]

## Planning for day one

Having greeted our children and organised name tags (essential), we would normally bring all our children to the carpet area for our first meeting together as a class group. Learning children's names is essential, particularly when we need their selective attention in any corrective context. Even before our – formal – day one we will probably have a 'photograph register' so we can normally learn their names by the end of the first day.[10] Sitting 'on the mat' (the front of room carpet area) is a crucial routine we will utilise several times a day – every day of our teaching life. It is easy to assume that children will know how to behave in this group context whether on the mat; in table groups; moving – when appropriate – around a crowded classroom. As with all the core routines we develop, we work with the children's natural, developmental 'readiness' (pp. vii, 37f). We also need to *teach* behaviour related to that readiness.

It is deceptively basic – surely – to expect children to understand what we mean when we say 'sit on the mat'? Perhaps not.

What we normally mean by 'sitting on the mat', is that we teach (and encourage) children to:

- Sit cross-legged; relaxed (without pushing back on to others), or sitting knees up and arms around knees. The *actual* sitting (in such a small area, 'cheek by jowl', is not easily comfortable if we do not consider personal space and place). It is easy to bump and push into, or across, another's 'space' on the carpet area. A *brief* discussion, and modelling, of these deceptively basic specifics help enormously. (This is crucial for children diagnosed with autistic spectrum disorders.)
- I once had a child who was so overweight he simply could not sit cross-legged, so those children who wanted to could pull up a chair or cushion (so as not to single him out). Naturally they would lose the privilege if there was any 'mucking around'.

■  Face the front of the room – and your teacher – and listen with eyes and ears. It is important that children learn to 'listen with their eyes' (p. 15). This helps *maintain* attentiveness (even transitory attentiveness!) This basic listening skill also (obviously) has wider currency than when the children are 'on the mat'.

■  Hands and feet in their lap or around legs (if the student has a strong – physical – preference for sitting that way). A key verbal cue we will need to use many times (in the first week) is, "Keep your hands and feet safe – in your laps." Never assume 4- and 5-year-olds know what a 'lap' is; explain and *briefly* model. Simple games are often helpful such as 'Simon says ...' for modelling close listening, body parts and spatial awareness. (See also p. 14.)

■  If a student wants to ask a question or contribute to the class discussion they will need to put their hand up (without calling out or clicking their fingers). One of most commonly cited distractions (noted by teachers) is *calling out* in whole-class teaching time; closely followed by *talking while the teacher is talking* (Rogers, 1994).

Some children think that it is 'OK' to call out, *as long as they have got their hand up*. In their minds they are 'obeying' the rule.

It is important to establish the fairness of the 'hands up rule' from day one. This means reminding children who forget, or those who are impulsive or overly attentional (p. 111f). We do this each time we have 'carpet time' (the class, together) on 'the mat'. A visual poster cue can assist children's short-term memory here. The poster is displayed on the board, able to be seen by all children. It illustrates how children have their hand up (without calling out or 'clicky' fingers). (See p. 19.) Children can be encouraged, and reminded, to think *inside their heads* before they ask or share. This is a behaviour pattern they will quickly learn and develop. After a week (or two) the *occasional* reminder is normally enough; often a non-verbal reminder (p. 54f).

Those children who *frequently* call out, butt-in, talk while the teacher is talking, or annoy others on the mat (pinch, poke, nudge ...) will need to be followed up beyond any normative classroom corrective reminder. The procedures for follow-up and follow-through are discussed in detail in Chapter 6.

## Establishing whole-class attention and focus

Once the children are 'on the mat' we have to assist them to settle, relax, attend *and* focus. Unless children can do this they will miss the essential features of any whole-class discussion and learning time.

## Communicating calmness

A crucial skill – in whole-class management – is the ability of the teacher to consciously communicate calmness to the class; as a group. This 'calmness' is communicated by our physical and vocal presence. Without attention and focus from the children we cannot – meaningfully – engage and sustain a learning environment.

I have worked with many teachers who, in seeking to settle, calm and focus a class group (for whole-class teaching time), will often add to any kinaesthetic tension by their verbal and non-verbal behaviour. I have sat next to colleagues whose voice has a volume, and 'edge', that is not only loud (and I do not necessarily mean shouting) – but actually raises unhelpful emotional energy.

You have no doubt seen those television advertisements where the presenter is waving his hands, moving 'zig-zag' across the screen, speaking in an abnormally 'hyper' voice, with 'Mr Bean eyes' all agog and hands waving as he seeks to exhort and con(vince) the viewers. I have worked with teachers who, while excitedly reading, or explaining pattern and order (in a maths lesson) or even 'morning talk' are *so* ANIMATED they actually 'wind the children up'(!) Many colleagues I have worked with are often unaware that their *degree* of vocal, and non-verbal body energy, actually *telegraphs corresponding energy* to the more restless children (unhelpful energy). When the children are supposed to be actually listening, focused, attentive (eyes and ears ...) and (yes) engaged – they end up being *over*-engaged.

A teacher's *characteristic* verbal and non-verbal behaviour is a crucial feature of their overall behaviour leadership. It is important to be *consciously* aware of how we normally 'come across' as the adult leader.

- How confident, assured, and relaxed do we appear, and sound (in contrast to hesitancy, abruptness, timidity or an arrogant 'self-confidence')? Can they sense our professional assuredness within our role?
- What kind of corrective language do we use in that whole-class 'settling-time'? Some teachers will overuse (or *characteristically* use) negative corrective discipline: "*Don't* talk when I'm teaching!"; "*Why* are you so noisy?"; "Do you *have* to do that?! Do you?" When a teacher characteristically uses these forms of language (particularly in an overly tense, or stern, or harsh voice), it communicates uncertainty in the teacher's role. It also *creates* residual tension in children; both anxiety and annoyance. Some children even interpret overly negative tone and manner (in our discipline language) as an invitation to negatively react back to their teacher. *Authoritative* behaviour is not to be confused with a bossy, *authoritarian* manner or a harsh, sharp, voice (Rogers, 2006).

I have worked with colleagues whose characteristic voice has a 'sheepish', almost frowningly pleading tone that appears to say (even to 5-year-olds), 'My teacher doesn't really believe what she says when she is telling us to be quiet, and listen …'. Children quickly – very quickly – pick up how confident a teacher is; how kind; how fair and whether they have a sense of humour and how far the teacher will tolerate or 'rein in' behaviour.

The need to present with a calm (not unemotional) voice; the need to speak *clearly* (and not in long complex sentences); the need to convey lift, mood and necessary energy in one's voice (instead of a monotonic, flat, overly sighing tone) is crucial in one's leadership communication.

'Calmness' is not inconsistent with the need for appropriate assertion – at times. (See p. 71f.) When we communicate calmness we are not conveying some passive, quiescent, behaviour; it is – rather – a respectful expression of confidence that seeks to invite co-operation from our children.

A helpful way to 'observe', or test out, your teaching style is to give the children 'free time'/'developmental play time' and then casually observe them. A group of children (usually girls) will go and sit on the 'mat' (one in your seat) and will proceed to play 'teachers'. They will have your teaching behaviour 'down pat'.

## Cueing for children's attention: whole class

As we scan the group we allow a little time for the children to actually settle in their place/space on 'the mat' (or carpet area). Our cueing of calmness will help in those first few minutes.

Some teachers use non-verbal cues such as clapping rhythm, or a bell; years ago I used to use a vibrant *strum* on my trusty Spanish guitar. One non-verbal cue we rather like (used by my wife – a former primary school teacher) is the *cue to head, shoulders, heart and lap*. Waiting for the initial settling of children sitting down on 'the mat' she then verbally cues the class, "When we come into class we think with our heads" (here the teacher touches head with both hands) "and relax our bodies …" (here the teacher touches both shoulders with her hands and demonstrates a relaxed breathing and sitting position). "We also think with our hearts" (here the teacher touches 'her heart' with both hands) adding – in a whisper – "and we put our hands into our laps to show we're ready to begin …" (she models hands/lap). The children then practise this several times. This, in subsequent occasions, becomes a *non-verbal* group cue whenever the children come onto 'the mat' as a group.

When we *verbally cue* (for whole-class attention) it is important to make clear what we are actually expecting. "Everyone ( … ) looking this way now ( … ) with your eyes and ears." The brief tactical pausing ( ... ) can help attentional take-up by children (p. 16).

> NB It really does not help to over-praise children who are sitting up straight (annoyingly 'ramrod straight'). "Oh! Johnny – you're sitting up SO NICELY!! That's great!" This is particularly important for children who *expect* over-praising; it is also unfair for those children who are sitting normally, attending, focusing ...
>
> The issue of praise (and over-praising) is addressed later (p. 76f). It is enough to *briefly* affirm and acknowledge children who are sitting appropriately and *then* engage the story, the 'morning talk' or the learning activity focus.

One of the phrases I find helpful in *establishing* whole-class attention is to say: "I want everybody to face this way and listen with your eyes and ears." If a child calls out – with a mischievous grin – "You can't listen with your eyes – ha ha ha!" it is enough to *tactically* ignore that kind of comment. On those occasions I have *refocused* the student's comment (without looking at him) by saying to the class group: "Some of you may be wondering how we can *listen with our eyes and ears*. Let me show you." At that point I will model the basic elements of attentional behaviour. We can also, of course, simply demonstrate these with a child at the front of the classroom.

It is also important to scan the faces (and eyes) of the group, very briefly and relaxedly, so as to connect with each child while we *cue* for whole-class attention. This enables the teacher to gain necessary non-verbal feedback (to see if they are listening and attending).

## Eye-scanning of the group

While this seems obvious – patently obvious – I still work alongside some teachers who either forget this, or are unaware that they are exercising a narrow visual focus as they address 25 (or more) children in front of them.

I have worked with colleagues who are utilising such narrow visual scanning they completely miss the boys pinching, pushing; the girls who are turning frequently around and quietly talking; the boy taking his shoes off and ...

This aspect of initiating, and sustaining, whole-class attention *and focus* should be a normal habit in teacher leadership.

- Scanning the group involves *temporary eye-contact* with each child. It demonstrates a connectedness between teacher and child, teacher and group.
- 'Scanning' also heightens a child's transitional connectedness to their teacher.

Even when reading a book to a class group it is important to pause (briefly) and scan for this 'connectedness'.

■ Scanning gives a kind of instant, non-verbal, feedback to the teacher. We can, often, sense if a child (or the group generally) is 'with us'.

■ Scanning also alerts us to any potential disruptive behaviour enabling us to decide what (if any) behaviours we can *tactically* ignore and what we will need to address. Until we get to know our class – as individuals – it is wiser to 'err' on the side of the *brief*, clear, positive, corrective reminder (p. 55f).

When giving verbal cues for whole-class attention it is unhelpful to ask the class group if they would face the front and listen. For example: "*Would* you please face the front and listen?"; "*Can* you please be quiet and look this way?"; "*Can you* please stop talking ...?" A whole-class direction is not a request; nor do we actually want an answer to the implied question (i.e. "Can you ...?", "Would you ...?", "Will you ...?").

A brief, simple, clear direction to the class group is enough: "Look this way everyone ( ... ) without talking ( ... ). This is our teaching time ( ... ). Looking this way and listening with your eyes and ears." Allow some tactical pausing ( ... ).

Thank the children as they settle ... "Sean ( ... ), Halid ( ... ), Zyin ( ... ), Chien ( ... ), Patrick ( ... ). Thank you for listening and settling quickly". Other children (at this eye level) will often 'pick up' on this brief acknowledgement and 'copy'. It will be helpful to then thank the whole class (as the class settles and faces the front). "Thank you everyone. You're all looking this way and listening and relaxed ...".

Children will – generally – rise to our expectations, providing we communicate those expectations with a calm, positive, expectancy in our language and manner (Chapter 4).

### NB  Tactical pausing ( ... )

You will note the ellipsis within brackets often used in the snatches of teacher to child communication in this text, *Tactical* pausing ( ... ) after verbally cueing a group, or individual (always by personal name), allows for cognitive take-up by a group or an individual student.

Sometimes we will need to repeat the child's name (or *group* instruction) to alert, and initiate, eye-contact and to sustain initial 'attention'.

For example the direction to a child who is inattentive and chatting to a fellow student while 'on the mat' (in whole-class teaching time) would typically occasion a brief, clear, direction. However we need to *initiate* the child's attention before any direction (or reminder) is given; tactical pausing enables that 'initiation'.

"Sean ( ... ) Sean ( ... ) looking this way and listening." As the child responds to the direction a *brief* 'thanks' is enough. 'Thanks,' is preferable to 'please' in most correctional reminders. 'Thanks' is more expectational than 'please' (which can often sound like a request).

*Tactical pausing* is essential in out-of-class contexts where we are seeking to establish eye contact and acknowledgement from a student over distance. The first verbal cue (often the child's name) may need to be said a little louder (without shouting) and then we drop the voice to a normal level when the child is attending.

## Sustaining whole-class attention

It is one thing to initiate whole-class attention, another to *sustain* it through the whole-class lesson activity; 'the class story'; 'the morning talk' ... As we sustain their attention, and learning momentum, we will often need to briefly discipline (by reminder or direction).

Some children will call out (while the teacher is talking) "Miss McPherson! Miss McPherson ...!" If we sense such distractions might merely be over-enthusiasm or forgetfulness, it can help to *tactically* ignore the distraction. Some children pick up on our *tactical* ignoring quickly and they – correspondingly – note the way we selectively attend to those children who put up their hand and wait – without calling out. When the child stops calling out and puts his hand up (no clicky fingers either) it is enough to say (when *we're* ready), "Michael ( ... ) I see your hand up. I'll answer your question in a moment. Thanks for remembering to put your hand up."

If several children have their hands up – again thank them, "Thank you for remembering our fair class rule. I'll answer you one at a time." We then nominate a child while briefly assuring the others that we will come to them in turn and they 'can put their hands down for now'.

It can also help to *preface* any class teaching time with, "I know some of you *really* want to share, and you may know the answer to a question *before* anyone else. In our class we remember to put up our hand and wait until I notice you. Then we *all* get a fair turn to share or ask a question."

In the first few weeks it takes children time to learn, and get used to, waiting their turn in a large group.

If any children are chatting while the teacher is talking to the group it will help to pause and – *briefly* – name and direct their behaviour.

"Sean ( ... ), Kalim ( ... ) – you're talking. This is class teaching time, (or 'story time', or 'discussion time' ...). You need to face this way and listen – without talking." A brief 'thanks' can often balance, and affirm, the correction.

If two children are touching each other (nudge, poke, push – 'testosteronic bonding') it is again enough to *describe* and *direct*: "Shannon ( … ), Paul ( … ). You're poking and pushing. Safe hands in your lap. Eyes and ears this way."

If the behaviour is potentially hurtful, or hostile, a clear – and brief – desist will be necessary: "Michael ( … ) stop that *now*. Move away from Sean and sit here" (teacher beckons to an area near to the teacher's chair). A 'desist' conveys a teacher's decisive '*stop*' message (see pp. 71–3).

Desists convey serious, firm, intent. They should, however, be communicated with a firm, clear, calm, assertive tone. After any corrective language to a child/children it is important to continue with the lesson or activity – to resume that sense of calm purpose. If children refuse to comply with directions, reminders, desists or relocation we will need to consider whether we will direct them to in-class time-out. This should be the exception (though not, necessarily, a 'last resort'). On some occasions we may need to resort to time-out as exit from the classroom. (See Chapter 5.)

## Overdwelling and talking over children

It is important not to *overdwell* when correcting children; "Michael, Sean, Patrick why are you talking? You know you're not supposed to be talking now don't you? How will you know what you're supposed to be doing later if you're talking now? Eh? No one else is talking are they? … Are they? …" Quite apart from the use of unnecessary (and irrelevant) questions ("*Why* …?", "*Don't you?*", "*Are they* …?") the teacher is *overdwelling* and contributing to potential restlessness in the rest of the group.

Avoid talking over any noise during whole-class teaching time or when giving *any* whole-class direction (say at cross-over activities or at pack-up time). This only habituates that it is (in effect) 'OK to talk, call out, or pinch and push other children, and surreptitiously annoy others while on the mat' (and *while* the teacher is talking with the whole class). I have seen teachers talk over – or 'through' – children chatting, calling out and fiddling (loudly) with *object d'art* such as pens, pencil cases, water bottles, rulers (etc.). They – then – (often) have to overly raise their voices. This adds to residual tension in the room as well as hampering *necessary* attention and focus by the children.

We have found it helpful to have a poster – already on the board behind where the teacher sits – clearly visible by the children.

The poster (see below) illustrates the expectations and cues (such as 'eyes – ears' and 'hands up and wait'.

We put our hand up and wait when we want to share.
We listen with our eyes and ears.
We take our turn.

## Whole-class directions

NB Whenever we give *whole-class* directions, instructions or even reminders it is important to go the front/centre of the room. This 'anchors' – as it were – the place and purpose of why the teacher is standing *there*: she is expecting the whole class to stop what they are doing; eyes and ears facing front of classroom; without talking. This enables the children get used to expecting *whole-class* directions when the teacher is standing at the front of the classroom.

I have (for example) seen many teachers give whole-class instructions to 'pack-up' from different locations in the room: "Alright everyone, you need to be packing up your pencils, papers – and scissors. Remember to put the glue sticks away *with the lids on* (!), lids on the felt-tipped pens because they'll dry out won't they? And makes sure there are no paper bits on the floor, and ..."

Quite apart from a ten-item instruction – the teacher is talking *while moving around* the room. She will be fortunate if a quarter of the class is actually half-listening. It is essential the teacher goes to the front of the room, cues for the (normative) whole-class attention and *then* gives the instruction or reminder.

## Seating areas (early years), for on task learning time

It is important to plan ahead (for day one) for seating arrangements: table groups, straight rows or split rows? The most frequent seat organisation involves mixed gender, 'mixed-ability', table groups. The key is not to *simply* let the children sit in friendship groups or *only* sit with their best friends; it is easy for 'cliques' to form (even at early years). The more restless and inattentive personalities are also likely to distract table group peers *if* we have not planned ahead who-sits-with-whom. It is worth discussing this issue with team colleagues on the planning day before day one with our children.

The least helpful seat-cueing (day one) is to say, "OK guys, sit on whatever table you want." Naturally the more gregarious children will tend to group with like-minded personalities and the more restless boys may quickly rush to the furthest table from the front of the classroom. Of course the children will need to know there will be times when we will sit with our friends in class time ..., but that decision is best left with the teacher.

### Seating space

Children will spend a lot of time in their table groups; apart from the uncomfortable seating often used in many schools we need to plan the formal seating arrangements thoughtfully. Test (prior to day one) the 'physicality' of seating space:

- Can a child move into his seat without distracting the child behind him? Most early years classes use table groups as their seating arrangement. I have seen children far too easily bumping chairs (inadvertently) because there simply is not enough space to move the chair 'back and in'. While this sounds basic (in print) I have seen far too many classes where lack of thought (and care) in seating organisation actually contributes to unnecessary bumping, which can – then – trigger disruptiveness and misbehaviour.
- Movement flow is also crucial between, and around, tables, locker-tray areas, and resource areas (for maths equipment, flash cards, games, library corner).
- Movement flow is crucial:
  – to, and from, the carpet area to the table groups.
  – to, and from, locker areas and table groups. I have been in classes where (for example) children's seating actually backed onto the plastic locker-tray trolley (where children kept their ongoing work and personal pencil cases, etc.).
  – to, and from, the coat/bag/hats area and (then) around table groups to the carpet area (at the front of the classroom).

Like any routine it is extremely helpful to discuss with early years colleagues how to plan and *fine-tune* these organisational details. By 'walking through' (as if a child), and around, these areas (in the classroom) one can get a feel for likely concerns. While we cannot plan for every contingency, we can minimise unnecessary problems by thoughtful *preventative* planning.

Name tag each individual seat/table space, chair and coat hook, and name label the normal table items such as pencil holders (keep felt-tipped pens away until needed!).

If tables are labelled (with an 'iconic marker' such as a primary colour, or animal, or something based on your current theme) this can help with grouping or direction (see over).

Seating groups will change throughout the day – obviously – as early years literacy and numeracy groups are ability based. Sometimes groups are even spread *across* the year level and will involve movement between several classrooms.

I have found it helpful to have groups visually cued up on the 'carpet poster board' at the front of the classroom. (See below)

It is then easy to say at then end of the morning teaching time, "Righto everyone ( … ) hippos are on the red table, giraffes are on the blue", etc. I have also used little icons to show the early years literacy activities they would be moving on to at 'changeover time'. For example:

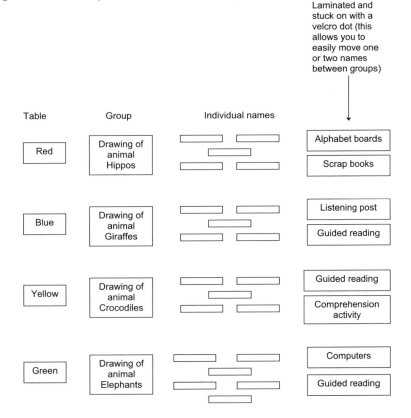

## Table groups

While table groups are probably the most common seating arrangement at infant level (commonly at new entrant stage), it is not necessarily the only seating arrangement appropriate at this age level.

Early years teachers tend to use table groupings to enhance 'natural' co-operative behaviour and social bonding. Such behavioural-learning goals, however, rarely occur fortuitously *because* of group seating! Teachers need to discuss basic behaviour expectations of table groups. They then need to teach *and model* those behaviours, and encourage and support such co-operative behaviour as they move around the classroom during on-task learning time.

If a class is particularly fractious (from day one) we may need to consider a more 'formal' seating arrangement (say split rows), and organise where particular children will sit (and with whom) for maximum co-operation and learning support. Again – it is always worth discussing these issues with our collegial team.

# Chapter 2

## Transition to on-task learning time

Many children at this age level find it difficult to sustain bodily, and cognitive, attention for long periods of time. I have seen teachers keep children on 'the mat' for 20–25 minutes (or more!) only to have to keep using frequent "Sshhs!" and "Stop talking" and "Be quiet!" in order to 'get through' that time period.

The amount of time children spend seated – *together* (*en masse* at the front of the room) – will vary with individuals' prior experience; *ongoing experience*; and (of course) age.

Ten to 15 minutes is ample (initially) to focus the group, and explain the learning task or activity or read a story. It is worth 'timing' ourselves in the reading of picture stories (or task explanations) beforehand. It also helps with some of the written forms of language in some picture story books which do not lend themselves easily and comfortably to reading aloud.

### Transition (between 'whole-class time' to 'on-task learning time')

When we direct children to go to their table groups (after whole-class time 'on the mat') it is essential we clarify verbally (and sometimes pictorially – on reminder posters) what we mean by:

- Working at your table group.
- Using an 'inside' or 'partner' voice.
- Where materials are (and how to use them). It can also help to appoint a table monitor for each table group. We can normally assess which children might be trusted (early) with the responsibility of being a table monitor (for paper;

scissors; glue; felt-tipped pens …). Later in the term children will have a number of rotated 'monitor roles' as they get used to the ebb and flow of classroom life.

- Use of water bottles.
- Toilet procedures (and 'leaving the room' procedures).
- How to get the teacher's help/assistance.

We never, ever, assume children know what to do regarding such routines even if we have actually 'told' them. The crucial *core* classroom routines for learning and behaviour are discussed later.

## Transition clarity

I have worked in many mentoring contexts where (as a mentor, team-teaching) I am not sure *when* the teacher has finished whole-class teaching and *when* on-task learning begins. There is a communal frown on the faces of the children; a muttering (*en route* to their table groups) 'What do we have to do again?' I have often thought, 'If I'm not really sure as an adult mentor-teacher what the learning task involves and *when* (and I was there; listening!) I'm pretty certain many children haven't "got it"'.

- Verbal cueing is less effective than verbal *and* picture/symbol/written cueing.
- Movement to seat cueing will need regular *positive* reminders, and a 'correspondence check' with children: 'What do we need to remember before we go to our table groups?' Even at this point (early in the first few days) enthusiastic children will call out (with their hands up). It is *always* important to clarify that if at any time a student wants to ask a question, or share, during whole-class time they remember *our* rule: 'hands up without calling out, or clicking fingers – and wait until (your) teacher calls on you' (p. 19).
- Noise levels will, naturally, rise when children move from the teacher directed and attentional focus of the whole-class learning time on the carpet area. It is crucial – each day – to remind children to use their partner-voices (p. 26).

It can even help to briefly 'role-play' some of the elements of 'on-task behaviour' before children move off to their tables.

Working noise, 'inside voices' (or 'partner-voice'), is a new concept for many children. Some will come from quite loud homes: television is blaring, the parent(s) – stressed – are shouting, even yelling (at times). Siblings vie for attention, space, place, time … Then, at school, we ask them to use 'quiet voices' in this classroom space with 20 (or so) children several hours a day!

We find it helpful to distinguish, and model, 'partner-voices' and 'playground voices' to children; and why in those places – and spaces – we use different *levels* of voice. We can even introduce the concept of noise 'volume'.

I have often modelled – in front of classes – a request from a student for (say) a red felt-tipped pen using a 'playground voice'; (a loud voice). Children invariably laugh. I ask them "What's wrong?" "It's *too loud* Mr Rogers!" I ask the class: "If we were playing handball outside would it be OK if we spoke this loud? If I wanted to 'have a go' in, say, a handball game?" I then model an 'inside voice' or 'partner-voice'. Using hand spanning, I then model the difference between (hands measuring WIDE) playground voice and 'partner-voice' in our classrooms (hands – now – close together). Some teachers find a 'noise meter activity' can also help visualise, encourage and monitor 'working voice' levels. (See pp. 26–7.)

> ### Simple, brief, modelling of routines and skills
> NB Even a deceptively simple learning activity involving 'cut and paste' with safety scissors can be helped by a demonstration, and inviting a few children up front of the class group (if they are comfortable) to practise with the teacher. We should never 'force' or 'over-cajole' a child to come to the front of the room and – in front of their peers – model, read, share … (for any activity). We invite. In time the more shy members of our class can be encouraged (privately) to 'try their hand …' in the public forum of their classmates.

## Noise volume in on-task learning time

The degree of tolerance by some teachers regarding the *volume* of noise in classes varies considerably. We have taught next door to classrooms where we can not only hear the 'distant' voices of many children but also the distinct, and very loud, voice (VERY LOUD) of the teacher. Should we tell them? How?[11]

It is essential to clarify with children what *we* mean by 'working noise' (day one and over the next few weeks). Modelling can be very helpful here.

- Distinguish between 'outside voices' (playgrounds) and 'inside voices'.
- Explain (and model) the *degree* of volume appropriate to partner-voice (how 'far' a voice really needs to 'travel').
- Explain, and discuss, that, "We are all together (20 plus …) in this one room. If we speak loudly, while we are working together, it's very hard for us to concentrate and learn (this can also be briefly modelled). When we use our inside voices it's easier for people to think inside their heads) and it's easier for me to be able to speak to you when I'm moving around to each table group …".

Some teachers find visual cues helpful in both the monitoring and habituating of 'working noise'.

Over 30 years ago a colleague and I (both with quite challenging classes of 7-year-olds) developed a 'noise meter'. As seen in the illustration, each quadrant on a 30 cm cardboard (laminated) wheel (with split-pin arrow) points to a picture illustrating:

1. *White*: when sitting together on the carpet area we are quiet; eyes and ears facing the front (and on the teacher. We listen with our eyes *and* ears); hands and feet safe; sitting comfortably (personal space consideration); hands up (without calling out) for questions and contributions (see p. 19).
2. *Green*: the children are using their 'partner-voices' ('inside talk'; 'work talk').
3. *Amber*: pictures the table group getting too loud, either by forgetting (it takes time for some children to 'acclimatise' to variant voice volumes) or by lack of any conscious effort on the children's part. This picture, when 'arrow-signalled', is a reminder to the whole class (not just one, noisier, table group). Sometimes children will visually cue to the noise meter (and arrowed colour) and can be seen nudging each other, "Look, it's on amber ...". As the noise

*volume* drops (back to a workable 'green level') the teacher will – correspond-ingly – put the arrow back on green (as if to say, 'you remembered – thanks'). She will then briefly thank the children for thinking about their voice levels as she moves around to each table group. The teacher, here, would cue the whole class (p. 19) and briefly remind them of partner-voices. The arrow is then put back to green. The teacher then goes to each table group to encourage, and refocus, work *with partner-voices*.

4. On rare(r) occasions if the reminder is not (at amber) 'picked up' by most chil-dren (arrow to amber), the teacher will stop the whole class and have a deeply sensitive, focused, caring nag … I mean whole-class reminder.

Our colleagues have used similar, visual cues such as little flags (coloured to cue noise *levels*); a thermometer-type picture going from quiet (green) to too noisy (red); student noise-volume monitors (at each table group); or simple verbal cueing. Any routine is an attempt to clarify 'why' a certain noise volume is important. What is always crucial is to explain the routine to the class group and *then* expect, encourage, correct (wherever necessary) and follow-through with children who have overly loud voices (see p. 87f).

## Getting teacher assistance (during on-task learning time)

Within a few minutes of moving from the carpet (whole-class teaching time) to their table groups (on-task learning time) some children are already calling out, "Miss, Miss … I don't know what to do …", "It's too hard can you help me?!" Some children will leave their chair and come over to wherever the teacher is and pull at their skirt/slacks, "Miss, Miss – help me …" "Miss …". (Even male teachers get called 'Miss' by 5-year-olds occasionally. When I do, I respond in a brief falsetto [Bill]; they soon get the message …)

### Parent/carer helpers

During small group tasks such as guided reading I made the rule (with my 5-year-olds) that you only interrupt if it is an emergency (the class joke example we used is that you only come and see me if you head is falling off). If children were 'busting' to go to the toilet the rule was, to come and tell me you are going (with someone else who preferably needs to go) and Velcro your name up next to the toilet picture on the carpet board as you are leaving the room. (See also appendix B).

This is when 'carer helpers' come in handy; helping by circulating and helping by reminding children what to do next; explaining instructions again; helping with computer glitches, etc. Good parent/carer helpers are invaluable.

## Whole-class prefacing

Before any transition to on-task learning time we need to explain to the whole class *how* to ask for teacher help and *why* it is important to ask (or seek) the teacher's help in the way we have nominated. We need to explain we are not 'an octopus' – we cannot be helping everyone at once.

The following whole-class prefacing reminders are essential:

"First we need to always check what we need to do for our classwork. Today we're going to be using this sheet (from our story: "There were ten in the bed and the little one said ...'). We will cut the sheet like this ..."

Having explained (and modelled) the task we also need to remind the children to:

- "... check the task, (the set work) – ask yourself this question when you're at your tables: 'What do I have to do now ...?"
- "If you're still not sure ask someone at your *own* table group." "I'll be coming around to each of your tables – anyway – to help you."
- "If you're still not sure you can ask me; if you want me to come over and help, you need to put your hand up (without calling out) and I'll come over as soon as I can."

  If several children have their hands up it will obviously be important to cue them, "I can see several hands up 'Sean', 'Troy', 'Zahreen'; I'll be around soon. While you wait for me to come over you can go on with ...", i.e., an ongoing activity, or task.

## Conditional directions

When children call out for 'help' (during the 'busyness' in on-task learning time) it can help (with some children) to *tactically* ignore – initially – to see if they pick up the implied message behind the teacher's 'ignoring'. More commonly we will use a conditional direction: "Cory ( ... ) *when* you've got your hand up without calling out *then* I'll come over and help you." "You're pulling at my shirt Janine. *When* you go back to your table, and hand up without calling out, *then* ...”

## Whole-class cues/routines

- The 'ask three before me' convention. This reminds children to ask others (at *their* own table group) before alerting the teacher.
- Some teachers – with older early years – use a 'teacher help board' (Rogers, 1998) – where children can quietly leave their table group and place their

velcroed name tag on a board. This – visually – alerts the teacher without the normal 'calling out' or 'hands up and wait'. Of course children need to have checked the task requirement *and* checked with a class peer first. They also need to know there are two or three options they can go on with *while they wait for the teacher* to come over to their table group.

■ It can help visual learners to visually cue the learning task with simple stick figure drawings and keywords or symbols. Some teachers have a smiley face with a hat on (the imaginary 'thinking-hat') accompanying the key task reminders. Drawing of scissors and pens all enhances the 'steps' (where necessary) to enable a visual understanding of the set learning activity.

I would more often than not complete any tricky cut and paste sheets (that involved cutting, folding, etc.) and stick the example on the white board.

For children on the autistic spectrum an individual (small) *personal* reminder-poster can significantly focus key learning steps or behaviour expectations. Such an individualised *aide memoir* will need to have been discussed and 'rehearsed' with the children – individually – before *any* classroom use.

## Classroom mentors

Classroom mentors are children who can be relied on, trusted, to effectively give some mentoring support to children with learning and/or behaviour disorders. When the class is well established (say three to four weeks) the class teacher selects a few children as available peer buddies/mentors to work alongside a child (when needed), or to sit on the same table group (and on the carpet area with) a child who has been identified as needing an individual behaviour management plan. (Chapter 6).

If any peer-mentor support is developed, it is important to clarify the mentor's role. For example, a peer-mentor will often be asked to remind their classmate (quietly, even non-verbally) to remember (say) to, 'put their hand up without calling out ...', to 'read – carefully – their worksheet', to use their 'inside work voice' (in comparison to a loud voice in class, p. 25). Some mentors will undertake this peer-mentor role with diligence, enthusiasm and empathy – it is important, though, that their own classwork does not suffer as a result. It will help if any mentor role is rotated among children with the necessary social and emotional intelligence to take on such a role.

## 'Pack-up time'

It is crucial to remind children about the need to 'put things back in the right place' (unifix blocks; picture story books – spine on left ...'; 'chairs *under* table, *on* the table at the day's end. This also teaches basic prepositions: in/on/under/beside/off/over ...). It is important to remind the children that in tidying the room up (at least at the end of the day) we are tidying *our own place and space* and we are 'doing our cleaner a favour ...'.

Not all children come from homes where there is basic tidiness. (Not the artificial, 'clinical' tidiness often irritatingly portrayed in those television advertisements!) There is no excuse for books just piled up in a corner, pencils on the floor, children' work left lying around at the end of the day (unnamed and undated ...); or a teacher's desk area impossibly piled with books, papers and a basic work programme (work programme?). Please excuse the cynical note here. Routine and organisation *enable* the smooth running of a busy place like a classroom – a learning community.

## Directions for pack-up time

As with any *whole-class* direction/cueing it is important for the teacher to go to the front-centre of the room and cue for settling/attention *before* communicating the pack-up routine (p. 19).

It is important to allow children *time to pack up* and get back on to the carpet area. Once settled – together – on the carpet area, then perhaps a song; a recap of some important feature of learning; reminders about tomorrow and notices to go home ... It is also important to have a dignified exit; nominating children through table groups, or simple 'games': all those with hazelnut eyes (hazelnut?; well ... brown ...), all those with magenta coloured eyes (well ...).

It often helps to give the children a specific cut-off time for cleaning up, and when it is finished they stand behind their chair and then I come around and 'inspect'; the tidiest table get their bags first and sit on the mat ready to go home. It is important – though – not to make this aspect of the routine competitive. The emphasis is on *normal* tidiness. We should consciously vary which group goes to the mat 'first'.

Some teachers find it easier if the children come to the carpet area (at the front of the classroom) *with* bag, coat and carer notices and – then – leave ('camel-burdened') *from* the mat to the door. Other teachers find it easier to dismiss small groups, from the mat, to the coats/bag area and door.

When dismissing in 'small groups' avoid phrases like 'those who are sitting so *nicely* ...'; 'those *good* children can go first ...'. There will always be a dozen, or so, children who will *always* sit thoughtfully, 'nicely', considerately. It is enough to give a reasonable and firm rotation of children (pairs/trios) from the carpet area. "Thanks Michael/Michelle, you're ready ..." is enough; with a goodbye of course.

Any fine-tuning of any of our *core* routines will need to be carefully thought though – collegial planning (as with all core routines) will help here.

## Colleague planning

The routines we have noted here are *core* routines; basic and essential to the establishment and *maintenance* of a positive learning community.

These core routines are best discussed, and developed, within our year teams. Our colleagues' experience, input, clarification, shared common values and expectations will help shape these routines and enable reasonable consistency across the early years department.

## Core routines and subject teachers[12]

There are some core routines that are helpfully passed on from grade teacher to each subject teacher:

- Lining-up routines (even specific language cueing that the year teacher has found helpful).
- Any *particular* seating arrangements (who sits with whom, and who should definitely not sit with whom!)
- Cues for any whole-class settling/attention.
- Noise volume cues.
- How to get teacher assistance during on-task learning time.
- Group-forming cues.

The subject teacher is not obliged to use these routines as such but why 'reinvent the wheel' if such routines are supportive, practical, positive and helpful? In 'handing over' and 'picking up' our class from subject teachers it is also important to mention (quietly) any *specific* issues of concern about behaviour and learning (particularly if a child is on an individual behaviour plan (see p. 113)).

## End the day positively

In the following picture I am counting down (at the end of lunchtime in class[13]) to table clean-up and off to 'lunch play'.

The 'pack-up' reminders are on the board. I am also singing (badly) a song "You are my sunshine …". I ask the children to nominate a song at the end of the morning (before lunch play).

Prior to the 'pack-up-song' is the 'I-can-see-your-lunch-song' "I can see a banana, a banana, a banana, A healthy yellow banana in your lunchbox today …" (We had been looking a the letter 'Y' – via 'Letterland'.[14]) "I can see some yoghurt, some yoghurt, some yoghurt …" (well you get the idea).

The last 'home-time words' should be positive – not manufactured *bonhomie* – but *positive* in tone. Rather than "You've been so badly behaved today! You've *really* disappointed me! I don't know why I came into teaching. Let me tell you …".

All the children want to do of course is get out of class and go home. Mind you – I have had a few children who have asked if they can come home and live with me! There are also parents and carers standing near the exit door (sometimes *too close*!). Some teachers then compound the negative end-of-day lecture the next day; they begin the day with the lecture continued. "I hope you're not going to be like you were yesterday! I went home with a bad headache and it was your fault. Well! Today you had better not upset me again …"

It is rarely the whole class anyway. It is unfair – and unnecessary – to verbally chastise the class group for the behaviour of half a dozen annoyingly behaved children.

## The last word to the difficult child

It is important that if we have had to exercise discipline in any significant way with a student that they go out to play and (more particularly) go home at the end of the day with a reassuring word – and gesture – from their teacher. So that the 'last word' from their teacher has the emphasis of some repairing and rebuilding.

## 'Lining up' (classroom entry)

Early years children have 'lined up' outside the classroom, in playgrounds, for as long as we have had schools. Any inherent purpose in such a routine lies in that conscious separation we establish (as teacher-leader) between children's social (play) time and in-class teaching and learning time. Some teachers allow children to haphazardly push, shove, elbow their way into a classroom noisily. It – then – takes the children longer to settle and reduce their kinaesthetic energy and playground voices. While social play is essential in children's emotional and social development, the classroom is not an extension of social play. Children need to learn we come into a different place, and space, and we are here for teaching and learning time. Of course we have structured play (and role play and imaginative play …) factored within class time, but the classroom is essentially geared for focused teaching and learning.[15]

It is also very important to explain (and show) our children where exactly we line up.

> As I was 'lining up' with a grade four class, I noticed Ibrahim grab Danielle's shoulder ('in-line') and pretend to knee her in the back. I was not sure if my colleague had noticed this (we were about to team-teach) in her class. I quickly (and quietly) asked her if I could have a quiet word with the class prior to classroom entry …
>
> I asked the boy and girl their names. I asked Danielle if she was OK. She looked a little nervous, but smiled, "Yes I'm OK". Looking at the boy I said, "Ibrahim, I saw you grab Danielle and pretend to knee her". (I modelled a very minor knee lift, and grabbed my own shoulder, to connect to his behaviour awareness). He frowned and said, "I was just joking!"
>
> Many boys will say they are 'just mucking around …' when they pinch, push, pull, elbow, pretend punch or trip … (non-malevolent 'testosteronic bonding' my colleagues and I call it). It is pointless to have a routine for 'line-up' if we easily overlook, minimise or ignore such behaviour – and the typical excuses (I was just joking!).
>
> I said, "Ibrahim ( … ) we don't ever joke like that in our class. We keep our hands and feet safe". He returned a sulky, knotted frown.

Looking back at the 'line' of children I gave a short, group, reminder about hats and sunglasses and the mat, and we went into the classroom.

*Any* routine we choose to establish is – hopefully – purposeful. That *purpose* will have been discussed with the class group. The degree to which any routine enables the fair, smooth-running of a class group depends on the relaxed vigilance with which we *maintain, consolidate and habituate this routine.*

You will always get those 'goody two-shoes' children who ask the playground duty teacher for the time and line up ten minutes before the bell. Then there are those children you will have to 'round up'. I have found it helpful to choose those stragglers on occasion as the 'line leaders' *en route* to specialist classes, thus giving them a chance to take responsibility and not be 'type cast'.

## Training?

As with any routine, or cue, or procedure (whether 'hands up', 'inside-voices', or 'pack-up' ...) there is an element of 'training': by this, we mean thoughtful initial explanation and *modelling* to all children. We then expect and encourage the appropriate behaviour as well as bringing correction – as the need arises – within the routine. In this way the routines enable a positive *habituation* about fair and co-operative behaviours.

### A note on lateness

When a child is late (a.m. lateness) it is almost always an issue of parental/carer responsibility. When a child comes in late (even in the middle of a story, or lesson) we should *always* stop what we are doing, briefly, cue the class ("Excuse me for a moment class ...") and genuinely welcome the child. We should *never* blame the child for being late, or add a scornful look (or word) to the parent/carer (if he or she is there with the child).

At the point when 20 pairs of eyes are watching this late 'entrance' we need to communicate a calm, warm, genuine and brief welcoming: "... Morning Jason welcome. Just put your bag over there. Thanks. Then join us on the mat. Come over here; sit next to Adam. Melissa please move over a little (beckon). That's it; thanks Melissa."

It is also important not to 'overdo' the welcome. Often a smile and a welcoming gesture to 'join us' are enough.

It is our confident, pleasant, welcoming tone that enables the late child's sense of inclusion; it also avoids over-attentional responses by the rest of the class.

If the child is frequently late (*very* frequent) it will be important that the principal (head teacher) has a private meeting (at school) with the parent(s)/carer(s).

## Summary: core routines

■ Organise seat plans and student groupings. (Table groups? Split rows? 'Who sits with whom?')

■ ENTRY to the classroom from outside: that cueing for expected, and *necessary*, differentiation between 'outside social time' and 'in-class teaching and learning time'.

■ Cues for coats/hats/lunchboxes/water bottles (when in the classroom).

■ CARPET TIME (after children have put hats/coats etc. away); the need to have a core routine for the group sitting 'on the mat'. Some children will need specific placement cues as to *where* to sit.[16] Attention/focus cues (to whole-class) need to be clarified, taught and maintained from day one.

■ Cues for questions/contributions in whole-group time. Hands-up convention.

■ TRANSITION ROUTINES. It takes children a while to understand, and habituate, the concept of class-*work* (or learning activities). For any meaningful on-task learning time we need to *clarify with the group*:
 – how we move from carpet area to table group
 – sitting comfortably (without rocking on chairs). This one takes a while for the more kinaesthetic child! (See also p. 121.)
 – noise *levels*/volume in this classroom
 – how to use table equipment (e.g., lids on felt-tipped pens straight after use, lids on glue sticks straight after use)
 – how to get teacher assistance for classwork *or* concerns about other children. In time children will soon learn that 'telling' teacher about every 'small' indiscretion (by other children) will not be overly reinforced
 – what to do with completed work (in time children will learn to date/name their own work)
 – leaving the room procedures.

All transition cues (from whole-class activities to 'on-task' learning time in table groups) need to be prefaced before we direct the children from the mat. Over a week or two these behaviours will start to become the norm and (hopefully) we will only need to give the occasional reminder.

## Peer support: first weeks

Some children cannot wait to start school. They will run in, full of enthusiasm, day one, without even a brief goodbye to their mum or dad or carer. Other children will see the school as a large, strange, confronting, confining and confusing place. They are anxious; some even 'fearful' of being left here.

Most of their normative socialising will occur in relationship with their grade teacher as well as their peers. 'Their' teacher forms a significant *in loco parentis* role. It is natural that aspects of emotional dependency, protection and security arise in such a setting.

In the playground it is a different matter. In that rough and tumble world, with big (very big) children – all that space, competition for use of equipment – the concern over friendships and social identity soon looms large for these shy, or anxious, children.

Many primary schools have a peer support (peer-buddy) programme in place for the first few weeks of term one. Children aged 9–11 are selected (and trained) to team up with a nominated new entrant or new to the school early years children (even in mid-term).

Peer-buddies are thoughtfully selected and trained in how to initially meet with their early years buddy on day one – first play period. They then walk them through the playground: showing them the equipment (and play) options; the sand pit area; the quiet areas; the board games/art options in the library …; the canteen (tuck shop); the toilets, managing school bags, personal belongings, lunch routines, etc. They will also link them up with other early years peers and often set up, teach and monitor, play activities.

A senior teacher is responsible for the training of all peer-buddies and will discuss – with them – the aims, and limitations, of their role and when to notify an adult if they have any concern about a child's welfare (particularly bullying). The peer-buddies – themselves – always have a clear idea of the sorts of concerns a 4- or 5-year-old has entering school for the first time. They are selected for their social and emotional intelligence and common sense. We often role-play how to introduce yourself to your 'buddy', how to reassure, where to meet, etc.

There is wide research demonstrating that such peer-support programmes correlate with the development of confidence in early years children, a positive sense of identity and belonging, and emerging resilience and social coping behaviours. There is also research indicating links between established peer-support programmes and school attendance.[17]

# Chapter 3

## Developing a whole-class child behaviour agreement

### The first days – establishing a classroom behaviour agreement

Erica and I sat facing her reception class. We wanted to review the rules and routines and develop with the children a *classroom behaviour agreement*.

We 'settled' the class down and said that we wanted to talk about 'our classroom rules'. Before we went any further we clarified the basic expectations of class discussion: 'eyes and ears facing the front', 'hands up without calling out or clicky fingers' and 'wait your turn. Thanks'. (See p. 11f.)

It is crucial to establish basic cues (routines) for any whole-class teaching time. Even on the first day when we discuss rules with our children we will need to *preface* any discussion by clarifying (even modelling) the 'hands up' rule. It is also crucial to give a reasonable time limit to student questions (or responses to teacher questions). If several children have their hands up – waiting – they can get bored or irritable. It is important to acknowledge, "I can see hands up. Yes Sean, Matilda, Erin, Paul ... Thank you. I've remembered you all. Hands down for now. Let's start with ...".

We then focused the class's attention to the three crucial questions:

- How can we *learn well* here?
- How can we *feel safe* here?
- What is *respect* and how can we show respect here? A sub-question here needs to also include: 'what are manners and how do we show manners to one another and why?' *Never assume children know basic manners* or what we mean by manners. Explain, discuss, model, expect and encourage manners (p. 5).

This whole-class 'behaviour agreement' is developed around three crucial, non-negotiable rights:

■ *The right to feel safe at school.* By this we do not simply mean physical safety such as pushing, shoving, tripping, use of scissors (etc.) but emotional and psychological safety. Issues such as teasing, friendship (and play) exclusion, lying, stealing, bullying all affect a child's right to *feel* safe at school.

■ *The right to learn*: children have a right to learn to the best of their ability; without undue or unfair distraction and disruption from other children, and with a teacher who cares about a child's ability, needs, their welfare and their self-esteem.

■ *The right to be treated with respect and dignity*, even when children are being disciplined and even when we do not (easily) like them. It is also crucial that we protect children when others infringe on their basic respect and dignity.

We do not, of course, use the word 'right/s' with young children; we do emphasise *right behaviour*. This concept of 'right' and 'wrong' is well developed by the time children reach school age. Children have learned to interface with rules and responsibilities (in varying degrees) from home, and their emerging sense of the wider social world, even through television (not always helpfully!).

Jean Piaget (in the 1930s) had researched children's developing moral reasoning noting the basic differences between 'autonomy' (literally a 'law' to oneself) and 'heteronomy' ('laws' affecting others). Children will often see the school as having some tension between their *immediate* needs and wants and others' needs and wants. As Piaget (1932) noted, this tension is normative and part of a child's social, emotional and moral development. As a child moves from home to school, from carer attachment to new (and significant) adults in their lives there will be natural tension about expectations, norms and rules.

Any age-related discussion about self and others is crucial in forming, establishing and maintaining a sense of 'rightness' in both a personal and social sense.[18] And while a child will often have sometimes 'black' and 'white' definitions of 'good' or 'bad', most children know it is wrong to steal, lie, cheat; they also 'know' it is wrong to keep interrupting a teacher while they are talking or keep calling out to get a teacher's help or to push, shove and snatch with other children.

Knowledge *about* (as we know too well as adults) does not mean knowledge *translated* into considerate and co-operative behaviour. This is social reality.

The skill of the teacher in establishing fair rules lies in keeping – and maintaining – a focus on age-related understandings of what is *right* and *fair* in relation to the critical areas of social relationships and school-based learning. This is why the *teaching* of behaviour is crucial in the establishment phase of early years classes.

While not all children will easily accommodate this understanding of rights and responsibilities, we will still need to exercise any discipline *within this reality*. Children need to experience the 'rightness' of fair rules and their responsibilities (and their consequences) – even if their home background and early learnings have not prepared them for a place like school.

## Whole-class behaviour agreements (or plans) for early years children

A *behaviour agreement (sometimes called a behaviour plan)* is – fundamentally – a shared understanding between teachers and children about fair, reasonable, safe, age-related, expected behaviour 'in our class'. The focus of the behaviour agreement is the individual class.

While its *formal* outcome is a published and shared 'plan' or 'agreement', it is the *process* and *practice* of what the document expresses and expects that will determine its meaning, its value and its utility.

A behaviour agreement – at this age level in school (4–7 years) – is as much for the parents/carers as it is for the children and their teacher. It is crucial that the class teacher discusses the related issues of behaviour and learning with her class – *in the setting of a classroom context*. Essentially the teacher is seeking to build a *learning community* based on a clear, shared, awareness and understanding of our 'rights' (as right and fair behaviours); our responsibilities, rules and their consequences. Of course at this age, and level of development (as noted earlier), we would not use those *terms*, though many children will be familiar with the concept, meaning, use and experience of *rules* and *responsibilities*.

In building a learning community the teacher will discuss with the class group *why* we need to think about which behaviours are right, proper and fair. The basis of *rights* are those values held as proper, appropriate, and fair regarding our behaviour here at school. Obviously this discussion is developed in an age-related way. My colleagues and I normally ask four questions to initiate and develop this classroom discussion:

- ■ 'What is 'learning'? (What happens when we come to school to learn?) "How can we learn *well* here?" This question often raises issues relating to turn-taking; hands-up 'signals'; listening to others when they are asking questions or sharing in class discussions; listening to others at our table groups; listening with eyes and ears ...; sharing equipment at our table groups ...; 'doing our best work', quiet 'working voices'; particularly discussing concepts like noise levels/volume. "There are a lot of us in this *one* classroom. We need to think about the difference between 'outside' and 'inside' noise." The teacher will, then, model 'partner voices' (see later p. 24f).
- ■ "How can we feel safe here? What do we mean by 'safe'?" (not only physical safety). This questions raises the issue of physical movement and our 'classroom space here ...'; how we treat one another; even the issue of positive language (see p. 51). Teachers often find it helpful to have a talk about teasing and bullying at this stage.
- ■ "What do we mean by manners?" Effective teacher-leaders never assume basic manners such as 'please', 'thank you' ..., 'excuse me' (when children move into/across another child's personal space); 'can I borrow?', 'putting things back after you have borrowed ...'.
- ■ "What is respect? How can/should we show respect to each other here ...?" This raises clear understandings, and behaviours, about *fairness*; *co-operation*; *consideration of others' needs*.

This sort of *guided discussion* helps clarify and consolidate *common* understandings and expectations about learning and behaviour. The focus on fairness and 'rightness' also gives a basis for the necessary encouragement and support of all children when they make the effort to consider others and co-operate with other children. Most importantly, the discussion process gives children a sense of collective ownership about 'our classroom plan' or 'behaviour agreement'. This discussion process will obviously need to be conducted over *several* sessions during the first few days. This allows take-up and some development processing of understanding.

### Classroom meetings

The ability of early years children to engage in group meetings to share, discuss, make judgements and decisions is well established practice.

*Nurture groups*, in particular, have been a favoured practice in Australian and UK schools for over two decades. The skills of listening, turn-taking; sharing thoughts and feelings and values; problem sharing and resolution are essential to personal and social growth. Such groups have also been utilised for developing understandings of restitution.

> Like any group meeting there needs to be clear rules for sharing behaviour (re turn-taking; respect of others' views; and listening to the speaker ...)
>
> Children develop these skills (in group meetings) like any other skills through guidance, opportunity and practice.

## Rules

When making rules with reception age children it is important to keep the rules simple, few in number, positive in expression and use inclusive language where possible: 'our', 'us', 'we', 'all', 'together', 'everyone'. It will also help to publish the rules in a large poster format, with a cartoon motif, and add (progressively) photographs of class members with 'hands up without calling out', 'working co-operatively', 'keeping our classroom tidy', 'using equipment safely' ... These photographs are then used in the published agreement sent home to parents/carers. Many schools use digital photographs of children to illustrate key features of classroom rules and routines. For example: a photograph of children walking in the classroom, with the words underneath, 'We walk quietly inside our classroom'. Another photograph illustrates a table group chatting and working: 'We use our partner voices in the classroom'. It is important to include all the children (in the various photographs) throughout the 10 or 12 pages that make up this behaviour agreement. (See appendix B.)

NB The use of digital photographs – in such home-school agreements – has wide currency. It should go without saying that *any* use of photographs needs to be contained with the probity guidelines of the education authorities and the school. Some schools (for example) use children's drawings instead of photographs. Most schools have substantial photographs on the websites. Using photographs within the *classroom agreement format* enables the personalising of links between class teacher, class and parents/care-givers.

## Behaviour consequences

■ At some stage in a classroom discussion on rules we also need to discuss *'what happens when we "break" the rules?'* What does 'breaking a rule' mean? What we seek to do, in these class discussions, is to help children understand the *related link between* behaviour and consequences.

Some behaviour consequences should be known in advance; those that relate to safety (scissors, fighting etc.) or those related to *repeated* distraction to others' learning. The most 'intrusive' consequence a teacher would normally use in the classroom is time-out (cool-off time).

Sometimes the teacher can *preface* the consequence of time-out to a student with a 'directed choice' that 'if' the student continues to behave in such-and-such a way (be specific) 'then' they will have to '*go to* time-out' (or 'cool-off time', or 'thinking time'). Five minutes is – normally – enough for a child to 'calm', settle, refocus. The teacher should always carry this through in a firm, but calm way; in a way that minimises any unnecessary embarrassment to the child concerned (see later p. 92f).

If the child will not (or 'cannot') calm and settle, we will need to consider exit and time-out away from the classroom (p. 94f).

■ The published document (the 'agreement' or the 'plan') will have a photograph of the teacher and the class on the front cover. If there is one document a parent/carer is likely to read it is one that has their child (and their teacher) 'on the front'. Photographs of children learning, asking questions, tidying up are also used throughout the document to illustrate aspects of positive student behaviour and learning. This 'plan', or 'agreement', would normally be published and sent home to parents and carers by the end of week one of term one, or (at least) by the beginning of the second week. (See appendix B)

I kept my rules laminated and in a spot where the children would see them frequently. Keep the rules simple and focused on the essentials. If you are using photographs of the children in your rules 'posters', it will be important to feature all children equally (parents/carers can get cross about those things) and obviously make sure you have permission to use the children's photographs. We put the rules on the wall where the children lined up, for a while they were under the whiteboard at their eye level. We also had rules in relevant places like computer rules above the computer, energy saving reminders on appliances and above light switches, etc.

■ Many primary schools use a similar *format* for their 'classroom behaviour agreements' *across all year groups in the school*. This gives a developmental consistency to the establishment phase of the year. It also gives a common understanding of 'rights', 'rules', expected behaviours and 'consequences'.

In this sense a classroom behaviour agreement is also a crucial feature of each class teacher's overall behaviour management and discipline plan. It is also an essential feature of a whole-school behaviour policy.

Children at each – progressive – year level also get used to the language, *and meaning*, of 'rights' and 'responsibilities'. They get used to the *shared sense of responsibilities and expectations* that such an agreement entails.

■ A covering letter from the principal should accompany this document when passed on to the respective parent/care-givers of each child in the class. This ratifies the document and gives a 'whole-school' sense of commitment about how the school perceives, and practises, behaviour management and discipline. (See attached letter pro forma later in appendix A.) It will also help to briefly define what 'our school' means by the term 'discipline' in *any* correspondence to parents/carers. In the letter we note that discipline is, primarily, the way we (as adults and teachers) lead, guide, encourage, support, direct ... children to thoughtful, considerate and responsible behaviour. *Any* discipline is exercised to help children to 'own' their behaviour as well as protecting the due rights of all children. It is not *primarily* about punishment, though the concept of *behaviour consequences* is a crucial part of discipline. Discipline has an *educational* purpose *and an educational focus*.

Thoughtful discipline is preventative as well as corrective; it also has a protective and preparing function as it relates to teaching children about their rights and responsibilities.

The classroom behaviour agreement (or plan) forms a *foundational* – and preventative – aspect to *all* our discipline.

## Subject teachers and the use of behaviour agreements[19]

All subject teachers will receive a copy of the class teacher's *class behaviour agreement* along with a list of core routines/cues used in that classroom. These core routines will address issues such as seating arrangements; cues for classroom questions; how to get teacher assistance; noise levels/volume during on-task learning time; pack-up arrangements ... Routines such as 'leaving the room' and time-out procedures *should be whole-school in policy and practice* (p. 94).

This will enable subject teachers to have an awareness of how each class teacher has communicated basic rules and expectations. There will, of course, be commonality across year teams about appropriate rules and expected behaviours. However, if an early years teacher uses a particular cue (say) for establishing whole-class attention – a clapping rhythm, a bell, a particular form of words – or a particular routine for 'working noise' or pack-up time, or a particular seating plan that has proved helpful ... these routines will help the subject teacher to have a behaviour leadership link to that particular class. This can, often, enable consistency and security for children as they move from year to subject classes.

# Class rules

NB Some rules will need to be situation specific, as when going out of school on excursions, or going swimming. Such rules need to be discussed, even practised (where feasible) beforehand and again, at the place of excursion, or the swimming pool, or ...

Rules overlap with routines. Rules and routines relate to each other as they focus on those crucial, and non-negotiable, rights about safety, learning and respect. Whether we are addressing *rules for behaviour,* or *core routines* for learning, and the smooth running of classroom life we always ask:

- Is the rule (or routine) enabling a safe environment, safe behaviour and supporting a child's psychological safety?
- Is the rule (or routine) enabling and supporting effective learning?
- Is the rule (or routine) enabling relational, social and environmental respect? (Rogers, 1998)

## Inclusive language (rule-reminders)

It is important teachers use inclusive language when developing and utilising rules: "We", "Us", "Our", "All", "Everyone", "Together". 'It is *our rule,* in *our class',* rather than '*My* rules' (as teacher), 'in *my* class'. This is not mere badinage; it emphasises the nature, and effect, of an individual's behaviour on (and for) others.

When using a rule-reminder (to a group, or an individual child) we will often express the rule indirectly, directly or in a question:

- "We work quietly (partner-voices) ..."
- "We share our pens, pencils ...", "We take turns and ask first ..."
- "Paul ( ... ) Adam ( ... ) What's our rule for partner-voices ...?"

The rule-reminder is the 'bread and butter' of our discipline. We will often preface such reminders with the word *remember*; "Mel ( ... ) remember our rule for sharing ...", "Alexander and Paul ( ... ) – remember our class rule for partner-voices ...".

It can sometimes help to express rule-reminders directly as a question, "*What is our rule for ...* ? (say 'partner-voice', or 'borrowing' ...)". The question encourages the child to *think* about their behaviour *relative to* the class (or school) rule. This form of rule-reminder is particularly helpful in non-classroom settings.

# Classroom rules/behaviour agreement

## Positive rules

It is not easy to focus thinking of the positive side of a rule. I remember having a discussion with a class about rules and each suggestion made by the children was consistently 'negative': "don't be rude"; "... don't run in class"; "... don't hurt others"; "don't chew gum ..."; "don't call out ...", "don't leave a mess ...".

I tried to engage their thinking about the *positive* nature of behaviour, "... many of you are saying what we *shouldn't* do. That's helpful; but how can we make the rule positive?" One earnest young lad called out (with his hand up) and said, "*Please* don't call out". And he meant it. We – eventually – got a shared understanding about *positive* behaviour; using examples and mini role-plays. When our class rules – and routines – are expressed more positively it often follows that the teacher's corrective language follows suit.

It is not easy – initially – to focus on the 'plus', or positive side of a rule. That is probably why some teachers' discipline language is expressed in *common negatives*: "*Don't call out* when I'm speaking ..."; "*Don't run* in the classroom ..."; "*Don't talk* so loud when you're working ...".

## Establishing rules

I have been in many, many classes as a mentor-teacher when teachers are seeking to establish their rules (or, in some cases, re-establish ...).[20] I have heard teachers say things like, "Well what rules do you think we should have in class?" There is often a 'sea of blank faces', or, a confused calling-out ... "Miss – we should be good ...!" or "... We should be quiet when we work ..." or "We should be nice to each other ...".

More often children will say what they should not be doing (see above). "We shouldn't call out!" (This while a student calls out with his hand up as if to say 'I'm doing the right thing'.)

Children need *guided and focused discussion* about rules, responsibilities and routines. They also need to understand, and comprehend, that such rules are there to protect – and enable – a safe learning community.

We obviously need to give children a voice in framing rules, but a guided voice.

## Consequences in the establishment phase

It is also important to discuss the *relatedness* of consequence to behaviour when developing the *classroom behaviour agreement*.

We ask the class some general questions about behaviour and consequences: "What should happen when ...?" (and the supplementary question 'why ...?'). For example: "What should we do if a student swears in class ...?", "... calls out lots of times?", "... annoys other children when they are trying to do their classwork ...?" (It will be important, here, to give a couple of brief examples.) Like all whole-class discussions, our timing is crucial. When we sense the attention, and focus, of the group is flagging it is important to draw the whole-class meeting to a close and refocus the class on on-task learning time.

The consequential link also has to be seen – by the children – as fair:

- If you choose to work loudly. If you make it hard for others to work (brief example is given) then you'll have to work by yourself …
- If you use any equipment (brief example) unsafely you will have to work without it, or do something else …
- If you damage equipment, you have to replace it (or do work to help pay for it …). This is a difficult concept at early years level but is an important concept to teach. Restitution (helping to make things right again) is a crucial concept to build into our behaviour management. It enables the child to develop understandings of personal responsibility and accountability, as well as empathy towards those they have wronged and hurt. (See later p. 107 and appendix C.)

  In all bullying incidents – for example – we would always invite (and encourage) the victim to come to a one-to-one meeting where they can face the perpetrator of the bullying, and make clear how they feel about what was said, or done, to them and what they (as victim) want to happen. This – of course – is conducted at a calmer, available time.
- If you keep making it difficult for us to do our classwork, hurt others, you will have to go to time-out (p. 92f).

It is important to let children know they will always have an opportunity to talk with the teacher – later – to help make things right. Like many aspects of discussion on child behaviour this is learned more in the experience of … than in the actual discussion of …

Many children will come from homes that have few, or no, consequences or excessive consequences. On deciding to keep one of my children 'down' an extra year I had an initial discussion on the steps of my classroom with the parents. I asked if they felt comfortable with him staying in my class again because I liked him so much (Elizabeth). "He's such a lovely boy" I said, "he always helps without being asked and is so cheerful etc." "What – this f—g little s—t?!" said the mother with a toothless snarl. In the background Kane accidentally knocked over a bottle of Coke on the asphalt of the playground and his father just 'lost the plot' with him.

I could see why our experiences with Kane were so different. He was thriving in an environment where he felt safe, happy, valued, etc. I 'kept him' another year – he was a great kid! It enabled that consolidation of core learning and social development essential in the first year of primary school.

# Chapter 4

## Developing a teacher behaviour management plan

## The key principles of discipline

As noted earlier discipline has a guiding and enabling function. Within our overall behaviour management discipline seeks to enable children to understand and 'own' their behaviour in a way that considers others around them. The degree to which those aims can be realised depends on how we characteristically exercise necessary discipline.

(i) *Discipline is grounded in, proceeds from, and is directed to a child's welfare.* Discipline in this sense is always grounded in our values. We do not hit children any more (thankfully!), nor should we use intentional embarrassment, sarcasm, put-downs, 'cheap shots' in order merely to control children or 'make them feel bad about themselves'.

When we use corrective language, we actually think about the *characteristic* words we use (and why). We also think about our *intent*, manner of speech and tone. This is addressed at some length later in this chapter.

Of course there are times when we need to be assertive; even to convey anger. We are even more acutely conscious, here, of thinking through (ahead of time) how we will convey our discipline in tense, disturbing or dangerous contexts (pp. 126f, 140f).

(ii) *When we correct we, therefore, avoid unnecessary confrontation.* A teacher sees a child playing with a toy during 'work time'. She walks over to the student and picks up the toy, "Right; I'll take that. You're not supposed to be playing now *are you*?" The boy starts to whinge, "That's mine, that's my

...!" He folds his arms and leans back in his chair – sulking. The teacher is even more annoyed – now – and the rest of the class (naturally) are attentive; some are 'excited' by the turn of events. This scenario happens in countless classrooms, even over 'small' behaviour issues such as this. In the teacher's mind she has to 'win', to show who is in control, and what is right. In the child's mind the teacher is being 'nasty', 'mean' and unfair.

In another classroom, a similar scenario – toy on desk. The teacher walk over, bends down on one knee to the child's eye level, and asks them how their work is going. (The *object d'art* is not mentioned at this stage.) After a *brief* chat about the work the teacher says, "You've got a toy there". The child frowns and says, "I wasn't playing with it". The teacher replies, "What's our rule about toys during class work time?" The student prevaricates (very common). "But I'm still doing my work." "I know you're doing your work Sean. Our class rule is, 'toys stay in our locker tray or bag'. I want you to put your toy in your bag, or on my table, until play time" (a *directed* choice). The boy, sulkily, walks off to put the toy in his bag ... The teacher tactically ignores the boy's sulking and when he has settled back at his table group she will go over and re-establish and refocus on the task at hand.

---

A direct question: "What ...?", or "Where ...?", "How ...?", or "When ...?" (relative to the student's behaviour) is preferable to "Why?"

The direct question "What ..." (often focused on a class rule or routine) enables a child to be 'behaviourally aware' and to take some behaviour ownership. If a child does not respond appropriately to the question the teacher will provide the answer (to 'what' or 'when') as a reminder or direction. (See also pp. 57, 73.)

---

The principle of unnecessary confrontation relates to any discipline context ... It shapes both *what* we say and *how* we say it.

There are times when 'confronting' a child is necessary. On those occasions we use our power, as the adult, in ways that are assertive (not hostile or threatening). We are also aware that children need to see – in our actions (as well as the rules) – where the moral weight of 'reasonable anger' lies. As the adult we get angry on issues that matter (hurtful, spiteful, behaviours such as teasing and bullying).

We use our power *for*, *with* our children not merely *over* our children. We do this when we keep our discipline *least intrusive* where possible (the example of the toy on the table ...). We only move to *more intrusive* intervention as circumstance, or need, occasions (as in use of desists or time-out consequence: see p. 71f and p. 92f).

(iii) *We use positive corrective language wherever possible.* Two children are fiddling with the window blinds during quiet reading time. Rather than merely saying, "Stop that now" (a 'natural' use of language perhaps), the teacher says, calmly, clearly, and briefly; "Adam ( ... ) Bilal, you're fiddling with the window blinds; this is quiet reading time." Even for five-year-olds this brief 'descriptive comment' is enough to raise 'behaviour awareness' and act as a reminder to appropriate behaviour. If the child appears (or chooses) not to understand, the teacher will immediately add a brief, simple, positive rule-reminder or direction. "You need to be reading your books quietly." She focuses, therefore, on the *expected* behaviour. She also keeps the discipline intervention *least intrusive* wherever possible. If they continue to fiddle with the window blinds, or chat ... she will clarify the consequence (sitting away, and working away) from one another (see p. 73).

When children call out, butt in, or ask to go to the toilet in the middle of story time instead of the simple negative "*No* you *can't*, it's story time", or "*No* – you *should* have gone at play time" (true – but ...), or "*Why* didn't you go at play time?" ... We can use a directed choice ... "When – then". For example, "When we've finished story time, then you can go to the toilet." The directed choice acts as a positive conditional direction.

A directed 'choice' is to be distinguished from the language of implied (or real) threat: '*If* you don't ... *then* you'll ...!'

(iv) *When applying behaviour consequences we emphasise the fair, respectful,* certainty of the consequence *rather than any* forced *severity.* Whenever we apply a behaviour consequence (whether immediately, or deferred) it is our calm, clear, and *reasonable* certainty that is significantly more effective than any shouting, gesticulating or threatening by a teacher.

(v) *Balance the short-term and long-term aspects of discipline.* We cannot address 'all' aspects of a child's behaviour in the emotional moment; in front of his class peers. Not the least because we have 20 (plus) other children to lead and support. We will – often – need to follow up any classroom correction with follow-up away from the child's class peers at the end of a lesson. (See p. 87f). Some children will also need longer-term, one-to-one support to teach specific behaviour (Chapter 6).

(vi) *Always follow up and follow through on the more serious and disconcerting discipline incidents.* When we follow up, and follow through (beyond the classroom time) we hopefully communicate to the child that:
  – 'Your behaviour is of such a concern it needs this extended time; this *certain* time' with your teacher (one to one);

– 'We care about, and for you.' Although we may be disappointed, even annoyed or angry at a child's behaviour we should not use follow-up time to berate or harangue the child (tempting as this sometimes is!) (p. 87f);

– 'Your behaviour is your responsibility but I can, and will, help you to understand your behaviour and make better choices.'

– In following up with disruptive children we also convey, to the rest of the class, that 'some classroom behaviour incidents are of such concern they necessitate this *detained time*'; there is an appropriate seriousness enacted here. The 'tribal tom-toms' soon pick this up.

## A personal 'discipline plan'

### Planning the language of correction

A personal discipline plan will involve clear rules and routines; a framework for behaviour consequences (including time-out) and even a *classroom behaviour agreement* (Chapter 3). It also needs to include a plan for our *characteristic* discipline and management language.

### The emotional moment

Often, when we need to correct a child (or group), the situation is somewhat tense; sometimes frustrating. Children pout, sulk, moan, whinge, answer back. The last place – and time – to *think* about what is more apposite to say, when we discipline, is when we are in that 'emotional moment'; when we are irritated, annoyed, tired, frustrated. A key theme – throughout this book – is the need to plan for discipline transactions as acutely, and reflectively, as we plan for any aspect of our teacher leadership.

### Positive language, positive tone

The degree to which corrective language is positive (in most instances) depends on tone of voice, teacher manner and body language, as well as the actual words (and nuance).

A teacher could use *positive words* – and phrases – when they discipline (and – clearly – not discipline *positively*). If such positive discipline *language* is exercised with a 'snappy voice', the gesticulating or pointing finger, the harsh or nasty tone, the degree of height (or bearing) ratio, or proximity, any potential for a co-operative child response is quickly compromised. Language is never separated from our *overall manner and intent*; this is more significant than words alone. Congruence between what we say and how we say it (intent) is what children take note of.

It is important to stress, again, that it is our *characteristic* tone and manner in our corrective language that children remember and respond (or negatively react) to:

- How *normally* confident, expectant, indecisive, non-assertive, clear are we …?
- How aware are we of the lift and tonality of the actual voice; that sense of wanting to engage with the class and the individual (bad day notwithstanding! p. 6)?
- Eye-contact is a deceptively fundamental feature of interpersonal communication. Stable, and relaxed, eye-contact conveys interest and expectation of co-operative response. Frowning, and annoyance (in our facial gestures), are natural (and normal) when we are annoyed or angry. It is important, though, not to *keep* frowning throughout in a discipline intervention. It will really help to relax the frown (beyond initial annoyance) as we seek to make clear to the child what it is he has done and what he needs to do in response to our discipline.

  It is important not to force eye-contact ("Look at me when I'm talking to you!"), particularly with children whose cultural background does not easily facilitate returned eye-contact to adults. With some children we may be mostly speaking to their ears (as it were). If they have a cultural (or behavioural) aversion to any sustained eye-contact we might need to have a private chat with them to clarify why it is helpful to look at someone when they are speaking to (or with) you … Any such chat needs to be engaged in in a sensitive and thoughtful manner.

  It is often enough to remind the children of the 'listening with eyes and ears expectations' (cf. pp. 12, 15).
- Balance the correction with normative encouragement so that the corrective moment is not *sustained* in a teacher's attitude beyond the actual discipline incident.

## More than personality

Teachers will sometimes say that the ability to exercise discipline effectively is basically 'down to personality'. I have heard this countless times.

While a normally positive, confident, expectant, relaxed manner will go a long way in enabling our authoritative leadership, we will still need to exercise such traits with skill. The skills of behaviour leadership involve organisation and planning as well as our *characteristic* communication. The skills in these areas can be learned.

## Non-verbal cueing

Non-verbal cues are a simple, quick, effective way to raise a child's behavioural awareness. A non-verbal cue can act as a brief reminder or non-verbal 'correction'.

Several children are calling out (during whole-class teaching time). The teacher simply raises her hand – and pauses – as if to say (of course) 'remember to put your hand up'. For those who call out *with their hand up* she adds a couple of fingers across her mouth – as if to say '… and without calling out'. This also keeps the teacher's discipline *least intrusive* (p. 50f).

- When Johnny seems to be aimlessly wandering during on-task learning time she calls his name (to establish eye-contact) and non-verbally cues him to remind him to return to, and sit in, his seat. She motions, with her right-angled cupped hand, a seat and motions her other hand 'into' the 'seat'.
- The teacher crosses her index fingers to cue for 'cross your legs' (this to a restless child on the mat).
- A teacher pointing to her ears and eyes cues to an individual child (or group) to be listening with their eyes and ears (see also pp. 12, 15).
- When a table group (or child) is overly loud the teacher briefly verbally cues the group (by name) and signals with thumb/forefinger to 'turn the volume down'. If the teacher is using a noise meter, the non-verbal cue of arrow to a colour (symbolising too loud) is often enough as a non-verbal *reminder*. (See p. 26f.)
- Many teachers use 'freeze' signals; non-verbal cues that communicate *stop* (whatever you are doing); *look* (to the front of the room) and *listen* (to your teacher). Common 'freeze' cues are the use of a bell and the teacher's raised hand (silently) that the children copy (raising their hand and looking/listening). There is also the 'hands on head' signal. The concern we have with 'hands on head' is it is quite uncomfortable and overly 'controlling' (contrast the use of a more relaxed hand-cueing signal noted on p. 14).

  Another common 'freeze' cue when children are using equipment (particularly musical equipment such as small cymbals, shakers etc.) is the two palm-outward hands cue modelled from the teacher which the children copy (so their hands are 'off' the equipment).

## Conditioned reinforcement

With *any* non-verbal cue used in behaviour management it is essential to set up the conditioned reinforcement by verbally cueing *while* using the non-verbal cue. We initially explain "what it means when I put my hand up like this …". After a few verbal associations we can then 'rely' on the non-verbal communication to carry the message.

> ### NB The finger
> Some teachers are quite unaware of how frequently they use the gesticulating, or pointing, or tapping finger. At the front of the room the teacher says, "You – yes Sean and Adam, don't talk while I'm talking". The negative tone is heightened measurably by a pointing finger waved in front of children's faces, or tapping on their work, "Why haven't you written your name on the page …?"
>
> When using corrective language it is important to be aware of using an open hand to emphasis our message in a non-threatening way.

# Corrective language

## Descriptive reminders

It is often enough to *describe* the distracting behaviour to older children; the brief description of a child's distracting behaviour is – itself – a corrective *reminder*. "Patrick ( … ) that's a loud water bottle." (This to a child 'cracking' his water bottle at his table group.)

"Sean and Hassim ( … ) you're chatting." (This to two children chatting during whole-class teaching time.) "A number of children are calling out." (This to several children calling out.)

Descriptive correction raises behaviour awareness in the child/children. For *some* children this is enough in terms of intervention; it acts as both a reminder and an implied direction. We have found this helpful with children as young as 4 years of age.

## Directional language

We often combine descriptive language and directional language. This is essential for younger reception-age children, for example: "Sean ( … ) you're calling out." (The descriptive element.) "You need to put your hand up without calling out."

A simple behaviour direction:

- *focuses on* the required, expected, appropriate or desired *behaviour.*
- keeps the language positive *where possible*. Compare the difference between "Don't tap with your pen while I'm talking" and "Michael ( … ) you're tapping with the pen (descriptive component). Pen down thank you. Eyes and ears this way" (the directional component). We direct to the behaviour we want/expect to see. "Hands up without calling out" rather than merely telling the children what we do *not* want to see: "Don't call out …", "Don't push in line …", "Don't fiddle with your water bottle …", "Don't answer back …". *Overuse* (not use *per se*) of 'don't', 'stop', 'can't', 'mustn't', 'shouldn't' are common features of negative tone in teacher discipline. We save such language for the necessary, firm desist, p. 71f.
- allows 'take-up-time' where appropriate. Take-up-time means we direct the student – then – and avert our gaze, or 'move away', to allow the student emotional space to respond. Take-up-time is not appropriate for *any* potentially hostile or aggressive behaviours.

Many colleagues have noted that changing their normal directional language from *characteristic* 'don't' to *characteristic* 'do' has made a significant difference in how consciously positive their corrective language becomes:

- "*Walking*, thanks" rather than "Don't run!"
- "Don't hold the scissors (or pen) like that. No wonder you can't do it properly. Here, give it to me" becomes, "If you hold the scissors like this (teacher models) it is easier to cut the paper …" "Now you try …"
- "*Remember to* …" is nicer on the ear (and more invitational) than "*Don't forget to* …". "*Don't forget to* put your hand up …" compared with "*Remember* our class rule for questions." (Teacher nods to the rule poster on the board.) We do not want them to actually *forget*; it is surprising – sometimes – the ease with which we say what we do not actually mean.

## Conditional directions

Michael (reception, 5 years old) was desperate to play with the farm animals on the 'play-table'. It was on-task learning time (about half an hour before lunch). The teacher I was working with allowed children to go to the play-table (or dress-up corner/shop) *when* they had completed their work.

I was working with the children at their table group; Michael persisted in his whining: "Mr Rogers, Mr Rogers … Can I play with the farm animals?" He was holding on to my shirt as I was talking with the other children. I *tactically* ignored him; he let go of my shirt, sulked for a while, then started again. "Mr Rogers …" I continued to tactically ignore him. A little while later I noticed him put his hand up. I excused myself from the other three children. "Yes Michael …?" "Can I go and play on the play-table?" He whined it out. I responded with a form of 'choice': "*When* you've finished your work … *then* you can go to the play-table. *What* do you need to do to finish this work now?" This kind of *conditional* direction has an element of 'choice' (always within the routines/expectations).

Other examples: when children want to go to the toilet in whole-class teaching time, rather than say, for example: "No you can't because I'm reading a story", or "*Why* do you want to go now?", "Why didn't you go at play time? You know you're supposed to go at play time don't you? – before you come into class?" (Many children get so involved in play, so engaged, they forget to go!) A mini lecture like this is pointless – particularly in front of the class. It is enough – now – to give the brief conditional direction, "You *can go* to the toilet *after* we've had our story (or teaching time)". Of course if we sense a child is 'desperate' we must let them go. Most children can wait until the more appropriate 'on-task' phase of the lesson. I have found it helpful to have 'fruit time' after lunch play. This was time during which the children went to the toilet if they needed to; then got some fruit (or any left-over play lunch) and ate on the mat while we had a settling story.

A conditional direction is also a 'directed choice'.

- "*If* you cannot work with your partner-voice, *you'll have* to work on another table."
- "*Yes*; I'll look at your work *when* you're back at your table group" – this to a child who comes over to get the immediate response of a teacher by pestering while she is busy working at another table group.
- "I want you to put the Barbie doll in your locker tray or on my desk ..." This to a 6-year-old girl abstractedly, 'secretly' playing with her 'little Barbie' during work time. This in preference to simply taking it off her table (or – worse – snatching it) "You know you're not supposed to have toys on your table in work time. *I'll* take that." I once had a teacher confiscate – and tear up – a 'teen-idol' postcard of mine (Elizabeth). I retrieved every last piece from the bin and taped it back together out of defiance more than affection for the postcard. I still have it somewhere.

NB The concept of 'choice' in discipline and behaviour management is important:

- It clarifies a child's responsibility
- When directions, or reminders, are expressed in the 'language of choice' the child is more likely to be co-operative. It can help, in some directed choices – with older children – to give some 'take-up-time' (Rogers, 1998). In the example of directing the child to put the little doll away (earlier), it can help to walk away (after giving the 'choice') *as if* to say, "I expect and trust you to do that". If the student does not comply we will need to go back and ask for the toy (not snatch). "It will stay on my desk until play time."
- It focuses ownership of behaviour, by 'if-then', 'yes-when, 'when-then' ... 'choice' language.
- It is important to express such 'choices' respectfully to invite expected co-operation. We do not express a directed choice as a 'threat'. All the examples noted here can be *heard* as a threat, or 'choice', dependent on our tone of voice, manner, intent and body language.
- A 'choice' (a directed choice) can also act as a conditional warning. Above all when a teacher is using the 'language of choice', thoughtfully, they are enabling the child to be an active agent in their behaviour.

It takes time for children to learn what we (as teachers) mean by such choices. This learning will come from how we *characteristically* treat the children subsequent to/contingent upon that 'choice'.

All 'choices' in this sense occur within the stated (and fair) rules and routines.

# Distraction and diversions

Two boys (six-year-olds) were playing sword fights with their rulers during on-task learning time. Not loudly, but annoyingly. I called one of the boys over, to distract him from his immediate audience. I gave him some take-up-time as I chatted with the other children I was working with. He shuffled over and stood next to me. "What were you doing?" I asked him quietly. "Nothing." "You were playing sword fights with your ruler" I reminded him. "We were just pretending!" (he protested). "Patrick (I made sure my voice was quiet, calm) I called you over here away from Thomas, so I could have a quick, quiet word." (I had, also, called him 'over' to briefly, 'privately', distract and divert.) "What are you supposed to be doing?" He briefly spoke about his maths work. "Are you able to do it? Does it make sense?" "Yeah" he frowned; then smiled as if to say "You're not going to growl at me?" "Alright you know what to do then? – and how to use your ruler sensibly?" He trotted off back to his table. Out of the corner of my eye (while working on the other side of the classroom) I noticed the lads chatting quietly (swords away). I also saw them look in my direction, and (with a wry smile) continue with their set learning task.

Typical distractions and diversions involve:

■ Asking a child a question, as a form of diversion, from their chatting (during whole-class teaching time). It is crucial – of course – that we do not do this in a way that ever intends to embarrass a child.

■ The sanity diversion, where we direct an overly restless, distracting, child to do an important errand: go to the library to get a particular book; or to the office with/for a particular message – always with a clear note. It is important not to overuse this 'sanity' diversion(!)

■ Asking a child to hold up a poster, a book, a chart/object *during whole-class teaching time*. We also need to avoid overuse of this as a 'reward' to the more restless/attentional boys. I had a lad holding a cup of tea for me once. "Two hands Liam and looking this way towards me as I read the story." He was consciously, and attentively, diverted – yet listening. I think he may have dribbled in the tea. I didn't drink it.

■ Children will sometimes call out things like "We done that kind of maths last year with Mrs Smith." The teacher *tactically* ignores this outburst, and without any visible eye-contact or engagement to that child, she diverts the focus and still addresses the substance of the outburst. "Some of you (she still does not make direct eye-contact with the 'outburster') might be wondering why we're doing number patterns again this year. Well …" Or she might ask *another* child/or two to share with the class 'What they did (with Mrs Smith) last year', relative to this maths topic.

- The most basic distraction/diversion is the non-verbal cue to the group when we want them to begin the pack-up routine: the rhythmic clap; the bell; the raised hand cue ...
- Invite a more responsible child to work with an easily distracted child (this 'diverts' the more restless child to task-focus).

## Question and feedback

Using direct questions: "What ...?", "When ...?", "Where ...?" raises behaviour awareness and enables a child to focus *directionally*.

Samuel (5 years old) was sitting on the table doing his work, instead of sitting on his chair – the other children (at his table group) were working on their maths activity and all sitting in their chairs. I walked across – kneeling at his eye level. I quietly described and questioned: "Samuel, you're sitting on the table ( ... ). Where are you supposed to be sitting when you do your classwork?" The thin, attentional, frowning whine (I'd heard from Samuel before), "I can still work like this". A little 'partial agreement' and refocusing of the task question: "Even if you can, *where are you supposed to be working*?" Before he could reply, another student (Adam) said, "Samuel, you know you're supposed to be sitting on your chair." Adam's tone was courteous without playing 'teacher's favourite'.

Samuel slumped in his chair, folded his arms, frowned and sulked. I had a brief, encouraging chat to each member of that table group (tactically ignoring Samuel). I noticed (corner-of-eye) Samuel starting on his pattern and order maths activity. I went over (a little later) and had a brief encouraging chat about his work. I could still sense his residual (attentional) pouting. I *tactically* ignored that aspect of his behaviour whilst keeping the brief – supportive – focus on the effort he had applied to his maths work.

Direct questions often focus on the rule, or routine, "What's our rule for partner-voices ...?", "Where do we put the felt-tipped pens when we're finished ...?" While it is natural to *just* tell children what they should be doing, a direct question requires the child to do *some* of the ownership of *thinking* about what they *ought* to be doing.

NB Some children on receipt of such questions will roll their eyes or sigh (as if to say 'I know, 'I know ...'). If they do not respond to the direct question we need to answer the question for them. Our answer (about what they 'should be doing ...') is – in effect – the necessary reminder or direction.

When we use a question and feedback approach: i.e., "What are you doing ...?", "What should you be doing ...?", "Where are you supposed to be doing now ...?",

"How are you supposed to use this equipment (i.e. scissors/felt-tipped pens/glue sticks etc.)?" – it is important that we use a genuinely expectant tone, not an accusing or threatening tone, or vacillating or overly 'cajoling' tone. It is always helpful to use a positive, appropriately firm tone in asking such questions. We ask such questions to enable the child's behaviour *awareness* and move his *thinking* to behaviour *ownership*. It is important to give the child an opportunity to actually answer the question. If they do not (or will not) we can answer for them. "This is what ... you should be doing ...", "This is *how* ...", "This is *where* ..." This, in effect, then becomes the teacher's direction.

As noted earlier, an interrogative form of questioning – in discipline contexts – is counterproductive. A question couched in 'Why ...?', "Are you ...?", "Should you ...?" does not enable behaviour awareness or call for any direct behaviour ownership.

Contrast, "Why are you being silly with the glue stick ...?" to "How are you supposed to be using the glue stick ...?" "What do you have to do ... (re: within set activity using the particular equipment ...)?" rather than, "Why haven't you started yet?"

# Beyond the 'primary' behaviour: *tactical* ignoring

Harry (aged 6) was annoying his reading partner in shared reading time. I called him across to me (away from his immediate peer audience). He continued to sit folding his arms; I called him again, "Harry ( … ) over here now." I turned aside to quietly address the table group I was working with and I noticed Harry 'come over'. His head was down, his arms tightly folded around his chest, and snorting (a difficult sound to write) – his pace accentuated by an emphasised stomping walk. He stood next to me; the snorting more subdued now. It is not easy – at this point – for the teacher to keep the focus of any discipline on the 'primary' behaviour that occasioned the choice to call him across the room for a quiet – clear – rule-reminder.

It is these 'secondary' aspects of a child's behaviour that teachers find wearing. When we address inappropriate, or unacceptable, behaviour some children will immediately pout, overly sigh, raise (or roll) their eyes to the ceiling (exaggeratedly at times); mutter (sibilant or loud), whinge, or moan, or whine: "It's not fair", "Wasn't me", "I'm not the only one …". It is these non-verbal and verbal 'secondary' behaviours that we often find as annoying (or more annoying) than the original – or 'primary' – behaviour we need to address in any discipline contexts.

## 'Secondary' behaviour

'Secondary behaviour' is mostly uninvited by teachers. Some children may be unaware of how typically, and frequently, they 'sigh', 'whinge', 'mutter', raise their eyes to the ceiling, toss their head in seeming insouciance …

Some children evidence 'secondary behaviour' as a 'performance' or to display attentional 'power'; for some it may well be 'habit'. It will help to have a one-to-one chat with the student about such behaviours (away from their class peers) (p. 51f). In this one-to-one context it can also help to 'mirror' the child's typical non-verbal (as well as verbal) behaviour. Mirroring *briefly* demonstrates to the child what their 'secondary' behaviours look and sound like. This is addressed later (p. 90).

When teachers are themselves unthinkingly rude – however – snatching, or grabbing, from a child (say a toy, or an irritatingly loud water bottle …), or speaking nastily to them, then a child's correspondingly rude tone, manner and body language are understandable.

## *Tactical* ignoring

It can help – in the immediate emotional moment – for the teacher to keep any corrective focus on the *primary* behaviour at issue and *tactically* ignore the 'secondary' aspects of the behaviour – the 'sigh', the 'rolling of the eye' … This is not easy. We are tempted to add, "… and don't you roll your eyes at me like that!", "*What* did you say …?" (this to the mutterer), "Why can't you just do what I say without whingeing!?", "You always sulk when I ask you to do one simple thing!"

Tactical ignoring is a teacher's *conscious* choice to ignore *some* aspects of a child's overall behaviour. It is a form of *selective attention* enabling a teacher to keep a clear focus on the main, or 'primary', behaviour at issue *now*.

If we focus (or more commonly over-focus) on the 'secondary' aspects of a child's disruptive behaviour we also give unnecessary attention, and shift the child's attention (and his peers'), from the *primary focus* of his behaviour.

'Ignoring' any aspects of a child's behaviour should never be communicated in a visibly 'superior' body language by the teacher. Children quickly pick up the difference. *Tactical* ignoring is a context-dependent skill. We should never ignore overt disrespect towards a teacher or student, or any *repeatedly* distracting behaviour (even calling out), or potentially unsafe or dangerous behaviour. On these occasions a clear reminder, direction or choice-consequence direction or command is appropriate.

The audience of peers (even five-year-olds) understands the difference in a teacher's *tactical* ignoring and 'blind ignorance' of repeatedly annoying distractions and disruptions by some children.

On many occasions I have had children grab my shirt *while* I'm talking/working with another child at their table group. "Mrs McPherson, Mrs McPherson!!" I sometimes choose to give no reinforcement; no eye-contact, no engagement at all – just the *tactical* ignoring. As noted earlier, this is not easy. It needs to be a context-dependent choice by the teacher. When the child settles and is 'quietly' waiting, or re-engaging with their work, I will *then* go over and give appropriate attention and support. I have had children say things like, "Why didn't you come before – I was calling out to you?" The helpful response here is to remind them of their behaviour and the class rule, "You were calling out (or grabbing my shirt) – what is our rule for asking for teacher help?" Our tone here is not accusatory but matter of fact.

## *Prefaced* tactical ignoring

There are occasions when we will preface *any* tactical ignoring, as when a child calls out several times. We respond with a rule-reminder or conditional direction and *then* tactically ignore any subsequent sighing, frowning or – even – calling out. "Paul ( … ) you're calling out. Remember our class rule." (Here the teacher non-visually cues, p. 54f). Any *subsequent* calling out by the child is then tactically ignored, the teacher having prefaced – by the reminder – what is expected. By not giving reinforcement (*tactical* ignoring) she is sending a message of expectation.

A useful form of language here is the conditional direction (p. 56f). In the example above of the child attentionally interrupting the teacher while she is working with another child, the teacher could give a clear conditional direction: "*When* you are back in your seat – without calling out – *then* I'll come and help you …" The teacher then tactically ignores subsequent calling out, and sulking, (unless it is extreme).

This is very effective in whole-class teaching and many children quickly pick up how their teacher is using *selective* attention. If the behaviour is in any way unremittingly repetitive/loud, and clearly distracting others, we need to intervene with a decisive choice/consequence or clear desist and rule-reminder.

Even very young children will have learned a battery of avoidance behaviours and avoidance language at home, with parents/carers, siblings, friends … Some children will respond to a teacher's direction or reminder with the 'clever' or 'smart' remark; or the tortuous and convoluted argument as to why "it wasn't me", or "It's not fair …", or "Others do it too!", or "My mum (dad, grandad, great-grandad, prime minister …) says 'You can't do that. …!'"

## Reframing

When children answer back, and seek to engage us in argument, it is important to *reframe* the reminder, direction, or focused question. We can help this process by a firm but polite 'blocking'.

We ask a student to go back to his seat, he has wandered off to another table group to speak to a friend; he is task-avoiding. We go over and direct him to go back. "Jarrod ( … ) you're out of your seat" (a brief, descriptive, reminder). "Where are you supposed to be now?" (a direct question) or, "You need to be back at your table group …" (a simple direction). Jarrod starts whining, "I *just* wanted to ask Dixon (his friend) for a pencil … (or whatever)".

The teacher addresses the child's 'explanation' by 'blocking' (as it were) and reframing, "Where should you be now …?" She does not *engage* with the avoidance 'explanation'. She also tactically ignores the whining tone.

## Verbal 'blocking'

A student calls out during whole-class teaching time. The teacher cues him (briefly) with a rule-reminder. "Carlton ( … ) remember our class rule for questions. Thanks." As she reclaims whole-class eye-contact, he whines out loud (arms folded), "Other people call out too!" The teacher does not get drawn into 'whether other children call out …', she verbally 'blocks' and reframes. "… Remember our class rule, thank you." She then continues the whole-class teaching focus and *tactically* ignores Carlton's pouting, and frowning and screwed up mouth …

- What we might 'feel' like saying is: "I don't care if other children are calling out! (we do actually). Which other children call out, come on tell me?! I can't see anyone else calling out!"
- "Well they were. Dean called out before, so did Romy, you didn't say nothing to them!"
- "Don't you talk to me like that?! Who do you think you're talking to ?!" The teacher is not just getting drawn into a pointless 'argument' – with a 5-year-old – she is also really annoyed by his 'secondary' behaviour (his overt frowning; his *tone* of voice; his folded arms; his 'defiant' look).

It is difficult at times to remember that we are the adult in the classroom.

If it takes argumentation and power struggles to 'win' with a 5- or 6-year-old *is it worth it*? – even when it 'works'? Utility is no proof of good behaviour management or discipline practice.

In some situations, it can help to briefly, *partially*, agree with the child. The teacher walks over to a child who clearly is not working (during on-task learning time). She greets him and acknowledges … "Troy ( … ) I notice you're not doing your classwork …". A little sulky, a little jaded, a little defensive Troy answers, "But I don't like this work." The teacher *partially* agrees/acknowledges, "Even if you don't like the work, it's the work we are *all* doing today. How can I help?"

As a visiting mentor-teacher (in countless classrooms – Bill) I have had children say to me, "You're not as nice as our normal teacher." One of my responses to this is to quietly say, "There aren't any *normal* teachers." The children do not always get my self-protective humour; some do. Another response I utilise is to say, "I'm glad you like your teacher. Even if you don't like me, I like working in your class. And I am a teacher just like Ms Smith …". At this point I then direct, remind or refocus the student to their work.

As with any *partial* agreement it is important not to sound 'defensive', or threatened, by an child's seeming (or real) rudeness.

As with all discipline interventions, if a student continues to argue, prevaricate, obstruct … we need to clarify the immediate (or deferred) consequences (p. 73).

## Rudeness

If a child is unnecessarily, or overly, rude in their *tone of voice* it will be important to let them know this is unacceptable. "Michael ( … ) I'm not using a rude (or mean or nasty) voice with you ( … ) I don't expect you to use a voice like that with me."

Our calm – slower – voice (here) is crucial. If we say anything (like the above) in an equally nasty (or mean, rude, offhand, sarcastic) voice, we have little moral ground for our discipline.

## NB 'Understandable cause'

Sometime a pupil's seemingly defensive, or argumentative, posture may have an understandable cause. If a teacher's stance is, itself, threatening it is little wonder some children would rail at the teacher. Thoughtful discipline aims for more that mere compliance, we aim for co-operation.

## When children are 'rude' to their teacher

Sometimes children will speak in a 'rude' or intemperate way, directly to their teacher. It is important this kind of behaviour is not ignored by the teacher (frowns, sighs, *sibilant* sighs and muttering are a different matter, p. 62).

When a child is rude in direct language (or loudly rude in tone of voice) it is enough to say, "Mark ( … ) I don't speak in a mean (or nasty, or rude) tone of voice to you. I don't want (or 'expect') you to speak to me in a rude (or …) voice". It is also important to establish eye-contact (wherever possible) and somewhat at the child's eye level.

As always tone/manner and eye-contact will convey our respectful, clear, concerned but *non-confrontational* intent.

### Avoid arguing as a way of resolving an issue of concern.

This is, of course, easier said than done! Craig (aged 6) is wandering around the room during on-task learning time. The teacher goes over … "Craig why aren't you in your seat?" (an unhelpful question, p. 50). "I was just getting a …; a …; a (he is thinking up a 'ploy') … ruler!" He was actually wasting time; wandering and annoying other table groups. I know; I was there.

NB. Children will often use "I'm *just* …" or "I was *only* …" to discount their behaviour, deflect or (simply) to excuse their behaviour.

His teacher was naturally annoyed both by his 'lying' (as she perceived it) and his argumentative stance. "Don't lie to me Craig – you weren't getting a ruler at all you were …". Here the teacher went into a long diatribe about what she thought he was doing. She finished with "… and you're just wasting time!" Craig has 'learned' how to 'stand his ground'. "I need a ruler and I was just going to get one!!" He has an emergent, sly, grin; it is this 'secondary behaviour' that is – *now*

– just as annoying as the primary behaviour of wandering and time wasting.

The teacher's voice is now – clearly – angry. "Don't lie to me Craig!"

"I'm not lying!!" Craig, only six, is willing to push this …

"Don't you speak to me in that tone of voice, who do you think you're speaking to?!"

A 'small behaviour issue' has now quickly escalated. It does not take long. Some teachers feel that they need to 'win' in such conflicts; they need to exercise *power* as a teacher-leader. The defining of behaviour issues in 'win/lose' terms will easily see a teacher's behaviour correspond to unhelpful beliefs about 'winning', 'control' and 'power' (p. 50). It is not a contest.

We are the adult.

The audience of peers is watching, adding to the teacher's belief about the need to show everyone 'who is in control'.

Yes – we have to control *this situation*, and we have to lead and direct the events with argumentative children. We do that more constructively and effectively when we:

■ Keep the focus of our discipline on the *'primary'* behaviour at issue (p. 62).
■ Avoid an unnecessary power-struggle.
■ *Tactically* ignore the sibilant sighs, and grins, and eyes-to-ceiling (not easy!). (See p. 62f.)
■ Always reframe any verbal rudeness.
■ Reframe the argument relating to the case example earlier (p. 64): "I've got a ruler here. *Now* where should you be? What should you be doing?" This refocuses the student on the task, or issue, at hand *now*.
■ If the student refuses to be redirected it is important to calmly, and clearly, clarify the immediate (or deferred) consequence (p. 73).

## When children 'squabble' or 'argue'

Children will sometimes (sometimes?!) squabble over who took whose pen/ruler/felt-tipped pen (or who *stole* their pen …!)

Children squabble over 'who said what …', 'whose turn it is …', 'whose friend is whose …'. After play time it is not uncommon for children to come in to class upset, annoyed, angry, crying because …

■ "Chantelle said she's not going to be my friend any more!!"
■ "Michael won't give me back my toy … Miss!"
■ "Jason hit me …!"

There is the natural busyness after play as children file into the classroom and we want to (and need to) get them settled, focused. It is important to balance the distinction between 'social time' and play time and – now – class time.

## First priority

The feelings (and tears) are real, and children are seeking our immediate attention and reassurance.

It is important – in the first instance – to acknowledge (and affirm) those feelings while making sure we do not get involved in who started what and why; *at this point. Now* is not the time to try to settle disputes or even counsel. When teachers do try to find out the truth, or *overly* reassure, it will unsettle (even confuse) the rest of the class. Some will even want to seek to defend – or argue – for the upset classmate. I have seen teachers standing in doorways for five minutes – or so – trying to unravel a sequence of events while the rest of the class mills around, some laughing, some wanting to join in, most wandering unsupervised.

- Immediately – but briefly – reassure the child/children in question. "I can see you are (both) upset (or annoyed, or concerned …) …" As children seek to rush out their stories it will be important to acknowledge … "I can see you've got a problem … we can't sort it out right now … go onto the mat … We can fix things later." It is important we communicate a reassuring and affirming tone. It is our reassuring calmness (and kindness) that they need to hear (and feel) at this point.

  When we use the word 'later' (to a 5-year-old) it may not mean to them what we obviously mean; it is a difficult concept for a small child. We will need to reassure the child/children that after whole-class time (on the mat) we can have a little chat; deferring any *involved* issues that may need to be addressed later.
- If the child is clearly, and visibly, distraught it will be important to send the child to the front office (with a trusted child), or give them a chance to sit away from others to calm down 'on their own', or with a responsible child while the teacher settles the class group.
- Squabbles and disputes in class time can sometimes be refocused within the understandings of 'sharing', 'turn-taking', 'sorting-things-out-at-a-calmer-moment'. If the issue has occurred outside of class and the child/children have (naturally) brought their concern, problems, anxieties into class time, then some cool-off-time is necessary anyway – before we seek to help the children resolve any conflict or concern.
- It can sometimes help (later in the lesson; later in the day) to give the children an opportunity to sit away from others, and quietly, work on some 'problem-

solving'. We will sometimes allow children to do this in a corridor area (where appropriate). Each child takes a turn to ask (and respond to) three questions:

– What do you think the problem is?
– How does it make you feel?
– What do you think we can do to fix things up?

A supplementary question involves asking – How can our teacher help us? Children are encouraged to work out a resolution and share it with their teacher at an appropriate time. This approach would only be considered if the teacher believed the children could cope with the questions/responses. Many colleagues who use this approach have the questions on a cue-card (with simple drawings to remind and use).

- Some schools train older children (9–11-year-olds) as 'peer mediators' to support younger children (both in class time and in playground settings) to engage in problem clarification and conflict resolution. These older children can be called on (even during class time) by the reception teacher to assist reception aged children to work through common concerns or problems.

It is important to remember that what may seem small to us – as adults – can seem disconcerting, even distressing, to a young child. By communicating to the class generally (and to children at times of concern or distress) that we have 'heard' them and will provide an opportunity to work through their concerns, we will assure our children that they can feel secure about sharing concerns, anxieties and problems with their teacher.

## The five-minute consequence rule

When children refuse (or seem unable) to share in a game or activity (where equipment has to be shared, or involves turn-taking) the five-minute consequence rule can help. This involves the teacher stopping the activity, recalling the equipment and giving an individual a refocused activity for five minutes, or directing children to work/play separately.

This is only effective if the class is aware of this 'rule-consequence' *and* the teacher telegraphs the consequence as a directed choice, "If you can't share or take-turns you'll have to work separately …".

## Swearing and 'bad' language

It is not uncommon to hear the dropped sh— or f— words; even at early years level. In one reception class (some years ago) a young boy said he wanted to 'have a p–ss' – in the middle of story time with the whole class. On another occasion he said (with a pained and strained expression), "I got to go for the s--ts bad". "Go" I said (he just made it!)

On the only two occasions I heard him use these expressions several of the class 'oohed' and 'ahhed' and one child called out, "Did you hear what he said Mr Rogers?!" I had a *brief* chat with the class about different words people use for going to the toilet. Later, I had a private, quiet, chat with Jayson about the same issues I had raised with the class. It is important not to moralise about language usage by children when such language is merely 'dropped' in communication or conversation, or arises out of normal frustration. We should – further – distinguish between any language (like that above) and language use that is used abusively *towards another* (including swearing). In these cases, a clear, brief, firm and assertive statement is enough: "We don't use that language here. It stops now."

All verbal abuse (swearing or racist) also needs to have careful one-to-one follow-up. It is in this calmer context that we can thoughtfully explain what is meant by particular words and the effect on others. It can also be helpful if the child is a victim of *any* verbal abuse, for the class teacher to set up an 'accountability conference' between the victim and the perpetrator; at a calmer, planned, time (p. 107f).

One of the naturally compounding factors with swearing is the mixed values and tolerance of swearing within a class group. Some children will practically never have heard words such as f—, or sh—, or a—hole, and will naturally be intrigued by, or want to experiment with, the language of their new classmates. Some children will hear sh–t and f— in parental/carer (and sibling) communication almost every day of their lives. They will also hear it frequently on television programmes; (PG: Parental Guidance means little – or nothing – to some parents/carers).

While we have no control over parental/carer values it is important (in a pluralist society) to give value to how we communicate at school without *judging the child*. It is also worthwhile having at least one whole-class discussion on positive language (particularly addressing swearing, put-downs and teasing language).

A quiet reminder or explanation is often enough, for example: "We don't use words like —— here." The *quiet, descriptive aside* can also help qualify – say – the difference between "I wanna go for a p–ss, or sh–t …" and "I need to go to the toilet …"

It is the same with the emergence of homophobic language used by some young children. Some children are aware of the *effect* such language can elicit (as too with swearing) even if they do not know what the words *mean*. Again the same clear, quiet, reminder is often enough.

One of the really annoying moralising phrases some teachers use is, "I don't care what language you use at home you will not swear like that here!" Quite apart from the fact *we do care* when children easily swear (or use put-downs), or use racist comments (even at reception level), it is a thinly veiled sleight on the child's family. Some children are sharp enough to pick this up.

With children who have poor self-control with swearing language (when frustrated or angry) it will help to develop a one-to-one plan with them to teach them alternative words to use when they are frustrated or angry. (See the framework for one-to-one plans in Chapter 6.)

It is often suggested that it can help to ask the child "what *that* means ..." (re: that *word*; the swear word a child used). The practical problem with this approach is if the child is angry he is not likely to always conceptually respond to what we *mean* by clarifying the 'meaning' of any given swear word. However, even in a calmer moment (one-to-one) if we say, "... do you know what *that* word means?" we need to consider carefully (as the teacher) whether we should use the actual swear word. It will hardly be helpful if a child goes home and says 'my teacher used the f— word today'(!)

It should be a clear, internal school protocol whether the use of a swear word (in this limited follow-up context) is appropriate, necessary or helpful.

It *may* help – to be clear to a child (one-to-one) – away from other children's hearing that some words are called *swear* words; words like (... here the teacher calmly uses the actual swear words typically used by the child). "... we don't use those words at school because they are swear words that hurt people's feelings ..." *Any* approach that countenances the use of swear words (even in a purposeful, *teaching*, way) should be authorised by senior staff as a teaching and 'counselling' option.

I had to explain to one boy which words were swear words as they were just a normal part of conversation in his home. On one occasion I said to him, "We don't use those words at school." He said, "Which words?" Then we had to go through and actually list them. Then there are those children (most often girls) who say things like, "Miss ... Jack just said the F-word!" "Oh yes; which word would that be?" "He said 'Shut up'!"

## Desists – 'stop – now'

There will be times when our discipline language will need to be 'more intrusive'; not hostile, mean or nasty but rather directly, explicitly, assertively commanding – in tone and manner.

Because our normal corrective language is least intrusive (in form, expression and language), when we use a firm and unambiguously direct tone, and language, children *sense* and feel the importance, and 'moral weight', of the behaviour we address (by contrast).

Matthew has pushed Michael, in the back. Michael falls over hard against his table. "Matthew ( … ) *stop that now*. You need to come over to me. *Now*."

It is not a request eg. "*Would* you *please* stop it now?"

Our voice is firm, clear – initially raised; a brief tactical pause ( … ) to initiate and sustain some eye-contact and attention. It is important not to shout. Having raised our voice (to gain attention) we drop it to a clear, firm tone …

It is important not to argue about who started what or whose fault it is. Those issues can be addressed later (with both children where necessary).

If the child refuses to come across to the teacher in a situation where their behaviour is unsafe or dangerous we will need to employ a calm, clear exit from the room. Any such time-out procedures will necessitate careful follow-through later that day (see p. 87f). It is also important – say when directing a child to time-out – that we do not negotiate with them, or cajole or plead (see p. 100).

It is not uncommon that when a student does respond to our desist that they evidence typical 'secondary behaviours' such as pouting, deep frowning, grunting, sighing and muttering, and – perhaps – the stamped foot. It can be helpful to *tactically* ignore such behaviour (in the emotional moment) and follow-up on this later (one-to-one), (pp. 87–91).

The audience of peers (even at age 5) can distinguish between *tactical* ignoring and blind ignorance! (p. 63).

*Tactical* ignoring of some aspects of a child's behaviour is a skill – a *context-dependent skill* that enables a teacher's discipline to stay focused on the student's 'primary behaviour', or issue, *at that point* and not get diverted into commentary on every frown, glare, mutter or sigh.

## Calm desists

Tyler was stabbing his worksheet with scissors. I turned, it was the noise alerted me as well as the disconcerting noises from the other children next to him. I was kneeling at the table group nearby to Tyler's table group. I walked over. "Tyler ( … ) put those scissors down now ( … ) *now*." In this case we need to use a calm, steady, firm voice (the scissors!) – no jumpy, jerky voice tone(!) If we put our hand out to 'take' scissors off a student, we extend the outstretched hand; palm facing up.

We should not try to snatch or grapple (unless there is extreme danger – this is rare). He slammed them down; a slight frowning grin (perhaps even an anxious grin). "Tyler, come with me. Cool-off-time." I beckoned him to follow me, as I started to move off (scissors in my hand). "But I'll be alright Mr Rogers. I'll be good!" (I 'ignored' his plea bargaining.) "Come with me Tyler." I walked away a few steps towards the cool-off-time area and he stomped over; following.

Once in the cool-off-time area I reminded him that when he had 'calmed down inside' (pointing to my chest and then my head) he could rejoin his table; without scissors for the rest of the day.

It is essential that we establish a cool-off-time area (even day one). The policy and practice of time-out is discussed in some detail later in Chapter 5.

## Deferred consequences

Sometimes teachers need to direct overly talkative children (who are distracting each other) to work at separate tables. Initially we will have briefly described their behaviour or reminded them of our rules, "You are speaking loudly. Remember our partner-voices (the corrective reminder). I'll come and check your work soon"; the cue to task-focus. It helps to leave children with a task-reminder (as above) or a task-question ("What do you need to be working on now …?" "What should you be doing now?") If, after some take-up time, they continue to work noisily we will need to clarify the consequential outcome with a *deferred* consequence (this gives some element of 'choice'). It can help to preface such a consequence with a directed choice/consequence, "If you cannot work here with partner-voices you will have to work at separate tables" (or: "You will not be allowed to work together, you will have to work separately …").

It is important *not* to phrase the deferred (but certain) consequence as a threat: "If you can't work quietly I'll move you!" It is the teacher's tone of voice and *intent* that determine how much the element of 'choice' is heard within a directed choice.

## "I don't care!"

On receipt of a direction that involves a deferred consequence we have had children say, "I don't care!" and sit back with folded arms, and a frowning, sulky demeanour. It is enough to calmly, clearly, note "I care" (there is an audience of peers watching/listening). Then leave the child – in effect – with the directed 'choice' *and the consequence*. It will then be essential to carry through with the consequence if the children continue to disrupt others' learning (p. 74). We may well be tempted to say, "You will care! I'll make you care if you don't do as you're told!"

One young man in our school believed in reincarnation, which I found out one day as I had a chat to him in his regular location – hallway outside the staffroom (having been removed from the playground). "I don't care what you do to me. I don't even care if you kill me, I'll just come back as something better." Well you cannot argue with that!

## Certainty not severity

Children learn as much from our actions – in relation to them – as they do by any corrective language (however well considered, and positive, that language may be).

If we go back to two very talkative children – having previously made clear we will direct them to work separately if they continue ... – and then give them a 'second chance' (in response to their 'plea-bargaining') we nullify both any element of 'choice' and fair consequential certainty. "We'll be good now – we promise! Miss – we'll be quiet!" "Are you sure?" (says the teacher). "Yes, yes ...!" they say. "Oh (sighs the teacher) alright then – but if you talk noisily again I'll have to move you." As she walks off the children grin to one another. They've learned.

## Respect

Respecting a child is not always easy; it will mean at least the ability to convey:

- Basic civility and good manners by *always* using first names; greetings; the smile (even to the 'unlikeable').
- Being conscious of a child's personal space (p. 80).
- *Always* balancing any correction with encouragement.
- Separating the behaviour from the person. At our best we know this as an educational axiom; it is not easy in practice with rude, intemperate, lazy, churlish behaviour. We may not like what 'our' children do, how they behave, but we seek to keep the fundamental respect intact whenever we discipline.
- Not 'keeping', or *nursing*, a grudge ...; and re-establishing working relationships with a child after any necessary discipline.
- Being prepared to apologise (even as the adult!).

Respect is not primarily concerned with how we *feel* towards a child or how we think we *ought to feel*; it is more about how we choose to relate to them – whether the child is easily 'likeable' or not.

*Any* sarcasm, ridicule or put-down undermines a child's confidence and affects their self-esteem. While the sarcastic comment is, I grant, tempting (at times) it is unnecessary, counterproductive and professionally, and morally, unacceptable.

Above all respect means treating your children how you would like to be treated – taking their feelings and needs into account.

# Caveat

## Repairing and rebuilding

Have you ever said about some of the children in your care, "I'll maim him so help me!" Most teachers don't mean that of course; they mean they're 'so frustrated that, that ...!', and emotion takes over – understandably.

Often emotions like frustration, even anger, are natural – normal. When tiredness, and juggling daily demands have to interact with squabbling children, slow (ever so slow) responses to our reminders, work not completed, arguing with us, squabbling, whining ... (you know!) Later – at the calmer time – you think "How could I have said those things?" Easily.

At times we do say the unhelpful, unkind, thoughtless even tactless thing; we get *too* angry. It is crucial on those days to repair and rebuild.

## Repairing and rebuilding is about:

- Repairing the strained, damaged, or hurt relationship (think about how they, too, might be feeling).
- Making clear that you were upset about (or by) their *behaviour*. Making sure they get the message that you still care for, and about, *them;* even if you were annoyed (at times even angry), with their *behaviour*.
- Distinguishing between mistakes, genuine forgetfulness, failure and active disobedience (we'd appreciate that if we were in their shoes).
- Making sure – as the adult – that we understand that problem resolution needs some 'cool-off time' before we're emotionally ready to confront the behaviour and fix things up. The child also needs that time too.

When communicating at a calmer time:

- *Use reflective listening* where possible, providing 'feedback' to the child: "Are you saying ...?", "Could you go over that again?" "As I hear it, you seem to be saying ...", "What do you mean? I'm not sure ...?" Try to keep the tone positive, inviting their co-operation.
- Emphasise what the problem is (without verbally 'attacking' the child): "What's the problem?" "How do you feel about it?" "How can I help?" "What needs to be done?"
- Avoid getting bogged down in excuses; emphasise that we (teacher *with* student) need to work on solutions.

■ We obviously do not have to agree with all that the child says or to condone what they've done; it is important, however, to reassure them that we care and show that we understand. Let them know how you see things.

Lastly, gain their agreement to work on a reasonable plan (or, at least, a better plan) for their behaviour. It may be appropriate here to discuss possible consequences for not keeping to any agreement/plan. See Chapter 6.

## 'Praise' and encouragement

It is axiomatic that children need, benefit from and actually require encouragement; however – do they need *praise*? By praise ( ... ) we mean that 'glowing', global, generalising: "Oh, that's *wonderful* Liam!"; "That's *great* ...!"; "That's *brilliant* ...!"; "That's *marvellous*!".

These global descriptors give no information to a student about their work (or behaviour). In fact they *over-praise the child*. When a child with 'low self-esteem' has expressed minimal effort regarding work (or behaviour) some teachers will say things like, "That's really *great* Sean – that's wonderful!" It is not actually 'wonderful', 'great', 'marvellous', or 'brilliant' because a lad (who rarely makes an effort) has written a sentence, or has sat on the mat without being reminded for the tenth time.

When we over-praise, like this, most children do not believe their work, or behaviour, is actually 'brilliant'. Or, worse, some children will only believe their work (or behaviour) is 'great' if we keep over-praising them in this way, telling them their work (or behaviour) is 'great' ...

The key elements of thoughtful encouragement:

■ Describe the child's effort, application, behaviour. For example, "David ( ... ) You've drawn sea mammals *and* land mammals and you have shown how they are different ..." "You've set out that maths sentence clearly Michael ... The numbers are set out in columns (the teacher points to the columns – reminding what we mean by 'columns' – the basic units and tens columns) – that it makes it easier to add up the numbers." Or the quiet encouraging word to the lad who (earlier) sat on the mat (without being reminded) and who put his hand up and waited his turn ...

■ Feedback – in this sense – is encouragement and is substantially letting the child know what we see, notice, 'feel' about their work or their behaviour (as their teacher). The descriptive nature of the feedback also enables the child to focus on *their* effort, thought, application ... In this sense our encouragement is not merely *our* approval; it strengthens the child's *self*-concept and (correspondingly) their self-esteem.

I was talking to a young lad about his art work. I asked him how he worked out his colours; how he had portrayed the tree trunk and branches and how he had illustrated the birds who were close to, and far away from the tree. I was – genuinely – interested. He smiled as he showed me his art work and clearly enjoyed sharing his work with me. A boy sitting next to him said, "Mr Rogers can you look at my work too?" I had not actually said his work was 'great', 'brilliant' or 'wonderful'. The other lad, too, had wanted to share his work.

- Avoid devaluing encouragement/feedback by adding qualifying phrases: 'if', 'but' and 'why' …

A child who often struggles with his writing produces several thoughtful sentences … The teacher notes, "That's very interesting Patrick … You have used lots of describing words to help us understand a summer day …" (helpful, so far, from his teacher). "Why can't you write like that all the time – instead of writing so scribbly?" This second comment underrates the first comment and may sound (to the child) like the teacher did not mean what they said in the first instance. It may well be the child will forget the first part of the teacher's encouragement. It is enough to genuinely note, and give feedback to, the child's effort, energy, application; without qualifying.

*NB* Age appropriate reminders about name and date on work are a different matter; they are task reminders.

It is often the *brief* aside that *recognises* and affirms:

- "That was thoughtful …" (here the teacher comments on how Sean helped Melissa pack up the felt-tipped pens and put the lids on).
- "That was considerate …" (be *specific* about what it was that was considerate, helpful, kind, generous …).
- "When you use your partner-voices (this to a whole-table group) it really helps everyone to concentrate. Thanks."

## Identifying with their struggle

"Alright, you made a mistake. How can we fix it? How can I help?"

"It isn't easy drawing a triangle. I remember when I was at school. It can help if … Do you mind if I show you …?" "Keep at it."

It is important to consciously make an effort to encourage those children who *always* make the effort to do their best. It is easy perhaps, to over-focus with our encouragement on those children needing more help and support in their learning and social behaviour.

## Recording

Many of our colleagues note how it is helpful to make a note of a child's effort (in behaviour or learning) – later in the day in a quiet moment. It is easy to forget (for example) how:

- Bilal tidied up without a reminder;
- Elise put the lids on all the felt-tipped pens so they would not dry out;
- Hong and Liam tidied up the library corner (all books, spines on left, cover facing front) without being reminded.

Many teachers – then – use the notebook as a reminder to share with both the individual (later) and with the whole class at the end of the day.

One of the more annoying comments heard by some teachers about giving encouragement is 'Why should we encourage children like this when they are supposed to be doing it (the work) or behaving responsibly anyway?'

The point of any encouragement is that it acknowledges and affirms (as well as confirms) a child's effort. We *all* remember the difference that genuine encouragement had on how we felt about our work or behaviour when we were at school, or university (or even as a teacher!)

## When children reject our encouragement

Some children will decry their effort when we encourage (or 'praise') their work, or behaviour. "I don't like it …" "It's rubbish …!"

We do not need to overly reassure children by saying things like, "I *really* meant it Melissa. It's *great*!"

Some children find it difficult to accept encouragement (particularly in over-ebullient expressions of praise, p. 76). They may feel they cannot live up to what we say is 'good', or 'great' or 'wonderful' …

Children will sometimes over-compensate against their feelings about failure or 'perfection' by saying, "I don't like it!" (their work) or even "I hate it …" Again – it is enough when the teacher gives a pleasant – assuring – "I think the work is …". Here the teacher briefly acknowledges – and describes – what *in the work* (or the child's behaviour) demonstrates thought and effort and leaves it at that.

Many teachers use home–school diaries – among other things – to add in brief encouraging comments about a child's particular effort that day in learning or behaviour.

For example: 'Jason has worked hard on his spelling words this week. I remember I struggled with spelling when I was at school.'

'Sean has consciously worked hard on his behaviour plan (Chapter 6). It has really helped him in completing his class work this week.'

## More than catching the student 'being good'

Teachers have – for years – been reminded (even exhorted) to 'catch children being good' in contrast to overly focusing on their poor (or bad) behaviour. In principle this is psychologically sound; children do (however) need correction and consequence as well as encouragement. The perpetual challenge for teachers is to enable the balance between *necessary* discipline and *necessary* encouragement.

Children with high attentional needs and distracting, disturbing attentional behaviours also need to be taught *how* to gain fair and appropriate attention without alienating their peers or adversely affecting the teaching and learning in their classroom and playground.

To do this we need to *directly teach* them alternative patterns of behaviour that can assist in meeting attentional needs but also enable effective behaviour and social skills. The strategies in Chapter 6 are devoted to the teaching methods we have found helpful to that end.

## Redefining labelled children

Some children will come to school with a self-concept affected by frequent negative labelling ... Phrases they have heard over and over again, often expressed in 'global' terms: 'never', 'always', 'won't', 'can't ...', 'just a ...'

- "He *couldn't* kick a ball straight to save his life!"
- "He's *useless* at ..."
- "He'll *never* learn to ..."
- "He's *just* (a) ..." ('annoying child', '... pest', 'difficult', 'lazy').
- "He *can't* concentrate ..."
- "He *always* fidgets ..."

Children's struggle with learning and behaviour is related to their self-concept (how they conceive themselves). Their self-concept is also affected by the characteristic ways they use to explain difficult, challenging or stressful events. This 'self-conception' is initially affected by how a parent, care-giver (or even some teachers) uses such 'labelling' messages.

When children are called upon to engage in the normal expectations of learning and behaviour, their concept of themselves is initially, and powerfully, affected by the confirming (or dis-confirming) messages they have heard countless times.

Haim Ginott (1971)has written that "A teacher's response has crucial consequences, it creates a climate of compliance or defiance; a mood of
contentment or contention; a desire to make amends or take revenge …
Teachers have the power to affect a child's life for better or worse. A child
becomes what he or she experiences. While carers possess the original key to
their offspring's experience, teachers have a spare key. They, too, can open or
close the minds and hearts of children." (In Rogers, 2006: 1).

What encouragement can do – in this new setting at school – is help children to
'see themselves' in a different light; *as able to* … School can provide a safe emotional climate where children have the opportunity, example, as well as direct
modelling and teaching to overcome their negative self-concept. It is in this way
that teachers make a significant difference to children's lives; their emerging sense
of self-value (self-esteem).

There are children who will 'test out' and challenge their new relationship(s)
with their teachers; to sense and feel 'how they belong' in this new place. There
are children who have experienced harsh, punitive, physical punishment who may
be uncertain, anxious or frightened regarding how a teacher will deal with their
behaviour. What is paramount is that children feel safe, valued and included. This
will depend – from the outset – on:

- How a teacher *both* encourages and disciplines.
- How a teacher validates and enables a child's expression of emotions (particu-
  larly anger) (p. 124f).
- How a teacher balances the rights of the individual child with that of the group
  (particularly with children with social, emotional and behavioural disorders).
- And – most of all – how a teacher enables a child to start each day afresh.

## Encouragement/discouragement

Comments like, "You call this neat, is that the best you can do?", "Why can't you
do this work? – it's easy, even David can do this …" are (sadly) not uncommon
even among some early years teachers. Even when the teacher 'means well' or is
trying to motivate, or is even 'speaking' nicely', most children will be discouraged
by such comments.

Moving into a child's personal space – without a thought as to how they might
feel – and just picking up their work and commenting on it is disrespectful; full
stop. For example: "You've forgotten to write down your name and copy down
the date! It's on the board …" I have had some teachers cavil at the 'suggestion'

they should (as normal courtesy) ask to see a child's work. It is *basic* courtesy – it also models manners when we come into a child's personal space 'invitationally'. "Sean ( … ) do you mind if I have a look at your work?" or, "I'd like to have a look at …"

These are not manufactured examples. I have seen (and heard) too many comments like those noted above. I cannot believe a teacher would intentionally speak, behave, in this way. It is to be hoped this is frustration and bad-day syndrome (p. 6).

Where such comments are a *characteristic* feature of a teacher's communication, such behaviour will need to be confronted, professionally and privately, within an understanding of considered and positive whole-school behaviour management practice.

# Chapter 5

## Helping children manage their behaviour

## Behaviour consequences

Children live in a 'consequential universe' – by natural default and also by design. They trip – they often get a bruise, graze or cut. They eat too much of the junk food and … They fail to brush their teeth (or get supportive home routines to support same) and … They lie and …

At home, and school, adults also 'design' and organise consequences related to distracting, unacceptable, unsafe, wrong behaviours.

Their world – as they develop – will confirm the nature and reality of consequences for their behaviour.

Children need also to learn that when it comes to behaviour it is not just about 'getting away with it', as contrasted to 'getting caught'. There are plenty of examples at home, on the television, in politics (later) that will blur their developing moral vision.

For now, at school, we seek to utilise behaviour consequences not as mere punishment but as the outcome of behavioural 'choice'. Some children are often quite impulsive (even in their 30s!) and it takes time to learn the correlation between behaviour and consequential outcome. We need to be careful, therefore, to teach this 'correlation' – particularly responsibility and accountability for one's behaviour.

### Basis for consequences

The basis for *any* behaviour consequences are the fair rules and their contingent responsibilities. In this sense a behaviour consequence *highlights* where a fundamental right (the 'right' and the 'fair' thing to do ...) has been infringed, affected or damaged (p. 38f).

## Consequences or punishment?

One of the points we often make in parent/carer discussions is that behaviour consequences are not *primarily* about punishing the child, in the sense of wanting him to purposefully *feel* psychologically hurt because of what he did that was wrong. As the children's teacher we utilise behaviour consequences as a signpost; a necessary part of the child's learning about their behaviour and the 'choices' they make (p. 58).

Even where a young child cannot easily see they have 'chosen' to behave inappropriately, recklessly, dangerously or violently, they will still need to experience the appropriate justice of related consequences. Fair – respectful – certainty is always a powerful teacher; more powerful than all the lecturing, nagging or vilifying in the world.

Consequences can, therefore, teach responsibility when designed thoughtfully and carried through with respectful certainty.

## The three Rs of consequences

The three crucial questions we need to ask about any behaviour consequences concern 'relatedness', 'reasonableness' and 'respect'.

1. *Does the behaviour consequence relate to the child's behaviour?* Many, of my generation, grew up with unrelated consequences such as 'writing lines', or the copying out of school rules, or empty detentions. In my case (Bill) physical punishments were the 'norm'. The 'hit'; the hair pulled (or ear); the cane; even standing under a cold shower (twice) because I failed to bring my P.E. kit. Ah! the good old days when we could *really* discipline(!)

    At my first primary school any swearing resulted in a mouth washed out with soap. My husband was locked in a cupboard (Harry Potter style!) (Elizabeth).

    We always need to ask how *related* any particular consequence is to the behaviour in question. Sometimes this is relatively easy (at least in 'design') as when a child has to effect restitution (p. 87f). In other cases we will need to help the child focus on the more 'related' aspect of the consequence. When a student suggests a totally unrelated consequence (say, "Not having my play time") we ask; "How will that help fix the book you tore?"; "How will that help get the scribbling off the desk?"; "How will that help you to finish the work you didn't do in class time?"; "How will that help Melissa feel better (the student you hurt ...)?"

This is where the key questions will help: *What rule* was broken? *What* can you do to fix things up? *How* will that help? And we should always add: *How* can I help you to ... fix things up, make things better?

NB. When we ask a child what they think their 'punishment' should be they will often be more 'Draconian' than even we might be tempted to be! We will often need to 'trim back' their excesses by the questions we utilise to focus their thinking (see above).

2. *Is the consequence reasonable?* There are two aspects to the concept of *reasonable*:

    (i) Is the child able to *reason* why a given consequence has been applied to him (to his behaviour)? Children do not easily separate out a concept like 'behaviour consequence' as compared to 'punishment'. It is important we enable the child's self-awareness (at the calmer moment). This includes tuning in to the child's feelings and giving them the opportunity to say how they feel about (and think about) the given – or 'negotiated' – consequence.

    (ii) Reasonable – as in 'degrees of seriousness'. The contrast between the consequence we effect for refusing to clean up one's mess in the classroom and racist teasing ought to be obvious. The school policy – and practice – will also clearly distinguish between non-negotiable and 'negotiable' aspects to any behaviour consequence. 'Negotiable' consequences involve the questions raised above. 'Negotiation' – in this sense – is always guided negotiation; focused on a child's awareness of their behaviour, the rules and why such behaviour is inappropriate, unacceptable, wrong ...

3. *Do we keep the respect intact?* We may well have a fair, related and reasonable consequence in place for a child but if we carry it through with disrespect we nullify any viability that the consequence may have for *teaching the child something constructive about his behaviour.*

Comments such as, "Well it serves you right!"; "I hope you'll learn now that you can't leave a mess and get away with it!"; "You shouldn't have done that should you!?" (they should not have but they did) "You're a very naughty boy aren't you?!"; "I'm sick and tired of your lazy, stupid behaviour!"

Stated baldly in print like this – it looks awful; we prefer not to think that any teachers would speak to children in these ways. We all get tired, fed-up and stressed at times.

Comments like this are – in part – understandable ("... you *shouldn't* have ...") but they do not help. In fact they often breed resentment or resistance to any constructive consequential outcome.

We do need to show our displeasure, even anger, at times; but not in these 'calmer' moments when we are actually 'applying' a behaviour consequence.

## 'Negotiable' and non-negotiable consequences

Some behaviour consequences are set by the teacher in discussion with the child. For example, if a child has damaged a piece of class equipment (say a book) the questions noted earlier enable the child to 'negotiate' (within the fair rules) what they need to do to take account of (and for) their behaviour (p. 90f). 'Negotiable' consequences are set by the class teacher based on discussions about common behaviour concerns at early years level. The key emphasis in any 'negotiable' consequence is to enable the child to 'think' through his behaviour – at a calmer time – and enable them to *work out* a way of taking ownership for their behaviour.

It is clearly not practicable – or workable – to have a stated consequence for every possible behaviour, though we have seen school behaviour policies the size of suburban phone books that try to cover 'every' consequential contingency(!) It will be important for the early years team to discuss the creative tension that naturally surrounds the exercising of behaviour consequences for repeated (but deceptively 'small') behaviour distractions such as calling out; annoying others at a table group; leaving a mess and refusing to help clean up etc.

Teachers can develop a *framework* of common consequential responses within the 3Rs principle noted earlier (pp. 84–5).

All grade teachers, in the early years team, will have discussed with their classes the basic nature of behaviour consequences in the establishment phase of the year. Children soon learn the *consequential reality* of what has been discussed in the classroom behaviour agreement, e.g.:

- When you push in at class line-up, or the canteen queue, you will be directed to the back of the line/queue.
- When you make it difficult for others to work ... *then* you will be reminded of our class rule. If you still make it difficult you will have to work away from others or have time-out.
- When you behave in unsafe ways, in hurtful ways, ... *then* you will have to have time-out until you remember and learn to behave safely ...

## Non-negotiable consequences

These are set by the school; they are set in whole-school policy and carried through uniformly. Any hostile, aggressive or violent behaviour, (including spitting at others, biting, kicking, or aggressive swearing) *any* repeated bullying will occasion *immediate* time-out (p. 94f). On some occasions there will also be a temporary exclusion from school. Sometimes we will use 'internal suspension; (from class) as an alternative to external suspension. *Any* temporary suspension is always organised with the senior administration team in consultation with the grade (and specialist) teacher/s.

These non-negotiable consequences should also be outlined in the parents'/carers' copy of the school's behaviour policy (see also appendix A).

## Follow-up and follow-through (after class time)

I was reading one of my favourite picture story books to a class of grade one children. As I scanned their faces, and read, I noticed (how could I not?) Bradley tweaking at a piece of Formica edging on the teacher's desk. Initially I tactically ignored it; the class was listening and attentive. A little later he pulled at it and it came away; he let go and the strip clicked back. I stopped, looked in his direction; "Bradley ( … ) leave the teacher's desk alone and hands in your lap. Eyes and ears this way now." I gave a brief extended eye-contact. He folded his arms, frowned, 'humphed' and went into a bout of minimalist grunting. I *tactically* ignored his 'elective mutism' (at this point) and continued with the story. "Eyes and ears this way class …"

A little later Nuyen put his hand up with some 'urgency'. "Yes Nuyen." His voice was serious; earnestly helpful. "Mr Rogers, Bradley's touching the table again." I had not noticed (though I did not disbelieve Nuyen's account). "Thank you for telling me." I eye-balled Bradley to let him know that I-knew-he-knew-I-knew-even-if-I-hadn't-actually-seen-him. I had mused (very quickly) whether I should redirect him to sit away from the teacher's desk.

He pulled at the strip again. I 'telegraphed' a consequence: "Bradley … leave the strip. Hands in your lap. If you can't sit there without touching the desk you'll need to sit over here." I motioned to a space near me. He folded his arms and grunted again. He did not touch the strip for the rest of the whole-class session. At lunch recess the children were back on the carpet area at the front of the classroom. I played a word game with the class and just before 'the bell' – and class dismissal – I said to Bradley, "… I'll need to see you after class for a little while." "What for!?" He whined and frowned and folded his arms. "I won't keep you for long," I said. He wanted to argue. I held up a 'blocking hand' and said to the class – "Well there's the bell. Time for playtime. Have a lovely time …"

I sent them off in pairs and threes. Bradley sloped off towards the door; I called him back.

"What?! I want to go to play now!" he whined; eyes averted and arms folded. I wanted to briefly assure him, "I know you do. I know you want to be outside with your friends. I won't keep you long ( … ) Bradley, come over here and look at the desk." I was conscious of keeping the voice calm and focused on the behaviour I wanted to address.

I crouched down next to the desk and looked at the torn strip of Formica. He came over; reluctantly. "Bradley look at that, you tore that off while I was reading to the class. And you clicked it noisily while I was trying to read our story (I showed him)." "A bit was off before!" Bradley whined it out. "Yes a little bit was off. (I partially agreed.) You tore all this off." I beckoned to the 30 cm of 'wavering' Formica strip. "How will you fix it?" I asked. "Eh?" He was not sure what I meant. I repeated the question. "It's damaged – how will you fix it?" Again, I was conscious of using a calm – even supportive – voice. "I don't know – glue it?" (He was thinking; less visibly upset now). I agreed that it needed gluing back, "What kind of glue? Do you think a glue stick would work?" He shrugged his shoulders.

I got some P.V.A. glue and we stuck it back, wiped the excess off with wet tissues, binned the tissues and sticky-taped the Formica edge back.

"I think that will be nice and dry and OK by the end of lunch play. What do you think?"

I had a brief chat about what I expected next time we were on the mat and added, "Enjoy your play time Bradley."

He sighed, frowned, half smiled and left.

James was refusing to complete his handwriting sheet. A particularly bright child, the poor kid was probably bored. None the less he needed the practice. I had walked past several times trying to help him to refocus (Elizabeth).

The next stroll past I noticed he was still no further along with his writing so I bent down, gently placed my hand on the sheet and said quietly, but firmly, "James, you need to finish your work." This tiny boy stood up, smacked me on the bottom and said, "I'm going to the principal and I'm going to have you fired." I turned around and laughed so hard I had to cover my face. There was stunned silence from the class, I think they thought I was crying. This boy was an amazing character, he would often stay and talk to me after school as I tidied up. I could see the bright, imaginative, inquiring lad beyond the task-avoiding and quirky threat to sack me! (For which we had appropriate follow-up away from the class group.)

## The protocols of follow-up and applying behaviour consequences

With any kind of follow-up and follow-through whether it be an 'after-class chat'; a brief restitutional session (as with Bradley); a behaviour interview (informal or formal); a detention; a time-out session or a mediation meeting, there are fundamental protocols that will *enable* behaviour ownership in our children:

- *Tune into how the child is feeling*; briefly acknowledge how they might be feeling at this point (staying behind after class, missing some play time). This both acknowledges and assures. "You're probably annoyed (upset or worried …) because I've asked you to stay back after class."
- *Focus on the issue, behaviour or task you have kept the child back for.* What is crucial in *any* follow-up with a child is the teacher's tone, manner and emphasis. We need to focus on the fair, known, *certainty* of the consequence rather than on any intentional *severity* of the consequence.

  I have heard teachers (even from a classroom away!) say things to children like, "Well you could be outside now couldn't you?! You're not, you're staying back, and do you know why; eh? You don't listen to me – that's your trouble. You've done no work this morning have you?! You've wasted my time – and yours. And what did I say Travis? Eh?! I said that if you didn't get some work done you would be staying back at play time – didn't I? And what did you say? You said you didn't care. You're caring now aren't you?!"

  The teacher's gesticulating finger (and natural frustration) is now replaced with folded arms and a direction to "Do your work *now*."

  Of course a teacher's frustration both during class time and – now – in the follow-up time is natural. However the teacher's behaviour (the language, tone, manner) actually creates resentment in a child, and works against what we (hopefully) intend: to emphasise behaviour awareness, accountability and responsibility.

■ *Keep the respect intact.* It is our *respectful* treatment of the child that will help to convey the fair certainty of the consequences.

In this sense we use the consequence process educationally, not merely punitively. While it is important in some consequential contexts to emphasise concern, displeasure, annoyance – even 'controlled frustration' – we need to do so with respect. Children will always hear our *intent;* whatever we actually say.

Some teachers think that by nagging (louder *and* longer) the child will 'get the message'. In fact it is the opposite (as many of us can remember as children!)

■ *Focus on the behaviour* – without 'attacking' the child. This is a crucial principle; and extends the points noted above. Keep the emphasis of *any* follow-up on the issue, the behaviour or the task for which you have detained the child/children.

It can sometimes help to *show* the child what his behaviour looked/sounded like. This 'behaviour-mirroring' (Rogers, 2003a) needs to be exercised with respect. The purpose of any mirroring is to briefly illustrate to the student what their repeated calling-out *looked* and *sounded* like during class time; or *how* they (kept) leaning back in their chair; or *how* they pushed in line ...

– Always ask 'permission': "Do you mind if I show you what it *looks/sounds* like when you ...?"
– Mirror their typical disruptive behaviour *briefly*.
– Physically step back; away – as if separating what you have mirrored of the student's behaviour, and that you are (now) the adult again.
– Refer the child to the 'mirrored behaviour', "*That's* what it looks like when you call out ..." (whatever). "Can you see how loud it sounds with just you and me here? Imagine what it sounds like in classtime."

■ *Right of reply*: where appropriate give the child a right of reply. This can be the simple question, "What do you want to say about ...?"

It can be helpful in an extended follow-up consequence (say a time-out session, or mediation session) to direct the children to express their right of reply in response to written questions. This would, of course, only be for older children comfortable with writing. It can also help ( with younger children) to ask them to draw a picture of 'what happened' and a picture of 'what they can do to fix things up'.

Written questions (on an appropriate proforma) would address: 'What happened?'; 'What rule was broken?'; 'What can you do to fix things up? Make things better?' We often add another question, 'How can I (as your teacher) help?'

■ *Refer the child to the classroom rules affected.* The child's behaviour will have affected how others learn, or feel safe, or have been treated. We need to focus on those aspects of the child's behaviour as reflected in our classroom agreement (p. 39f). It is important to do this briefly, and clearly, with a focus on *our* classroom rules. In some extended one-to-one sessions we will need to work constructively with the child on some kind of individual behaviour plan (p. 113). In an after-class chat it is enough to clarify – again – the expected behaviour (relevant to this follow-up).

■ *Separate amicably.* We show the child (by our tone and manner) that we hold no grudges; that we accept them (having addressed our concern about their behaviour and our expectation about the future). We do not, at this point, dwell on the child's immediate past behaviour.

"You do that again; you speak to me like that again and you won't just be speaking to me! – or the Principal! Or your mother! I'll …" (We'll what? – ring the Minister for Education?)

We do not need to *re*-lecture the child (as if to 'cement home' the seriousness of their behaviour). All that does is reawaken residual tension and even the resentment that will resurface later.

It is enough to say, "Enjoy your play time Bradley. See you later." Difficult as it is at times to remember: we are the adult – they are the child.

NB If we have had to follow-up with a child several times for similar behaviour issues it will be crucial to develop an *individual behaviour plan* with them. This is addressed in some detail in Chapter 6.

Remember when you are dealing with those difficult children (the ones you sometimes hope will be absent at morning roll call), that they may one day:

■ Be a parent or teacher themselves.
■ They may even be the doctor that cures your illness or disease.
■ They may well be the car thief that you have them pegged for (but don't think about that!)

## When children run off

I was taking 'my' 6–7-year-olds into class (many years back now) and the 'most challenging lad' 'did a runner'. The bell had gone and I had called the class over to where we all 'lined up' after play. He came, but then (for attentional 'fun') ran off to the climbing frame shrieking with laughter. It was not the first time.

Fortunately at this school we had a clear protocol for this event and for children who refused to come in (off the play equipment) when we are 'lining up' our classes. When Sean 'did a runner' I sent one of my 'trusted children' to the front office with the red card; a small, laminated, red card with our classroom number on. When any senior teacher (at the admin.) received such a card it meant 'there-is-a-major-issue-of-concern-or-crisis-in-or-around-room-17 ... please-come-straight-away!' We did not have mobile phones back then (Bill).

What is essential (when a child 'does a runner') is that we stay with our class. We have a legal duty-of-care to stay with the class and to *immediately* notify the administration.

With children who run off frequently (in such settings) we will need to set up an *individual behaviour plan* to address the required behaviour (Chapter 6). This plan needs parental understanding and support.

## Time-out

At this age there are children who have poorly developed frustration-tolerance behaviours. Their low tolerance to frustration may see them quickly, 'easily', lash out at others if they cannot get their 'own way', or if they are frustrated in their learning task expectations.

Time-out is *part of* the learning that such feelings (frustration and anger) are not bad in themselves (an axiom true of any emotion simply *as* an emotion). It is what one *does (*characteristically*)* with emotions that matters; this is *learned behaviour.*

When children hit out in anger ...; spit at others; push over children (or furniture); throw things; kick ...; bite ...; they need to 'learn' that such behaviour will not be tolerated (however difficult the child's out of school life). TIME-OUT (at least) sets up an association of *when – then*: 'When you hurt others, or *keep* making it difficult for others to learn, you will have to face time-out (time away from your class peers) until you can calm down, settle and think about how you need to behave *here* (in *our* class)'.

This is an associative form of learning and while it does not directly teach the child – long-term – how he ought to behave, time-out enables a clear, safe, and *necessary* link in the behaviour-learning process.

We should always follow-up *any* time-out with repairing and rebuilding (p. 75f).

Beyond any one-to-one dialogue there will often need to be some kind of restitution, as when a child has been verbally, or physically, abusive to another child; or to direct the child to catch-up time if a child's classwork has been significantly affected by his time in time-out. Some children will need a *personal* behaviour plan if they are frequently in time-out (see Chapter 6).

It needs to be stressed – again – that even if the child has had very poor modelling (from home), or has a diagnosed behaviour disorder, this does not *excuse* his behaviour in the group setting. While a child's behaviour may be explained (in significant part) by 'causative pathology' (p. 109) it should not excuse significantly disruptive (or dangerous) behaviours. Nor should it excuse necessary discipline procedures and processes to enable the child's accountability.

It is also crucial that the audience of peers see some correlative justice in a teacher's application of time-out.

Having said that, some behaviours do need to be 'excused' in the sense that we need to be acutely aware of prevailing factors. One 5-year-old boy I taught from the 'commission flats'[21] used to fall asleep after lunch (as he was often seen out until all hours on the streets and basketball courts). I would put a pillow under his head, a blanket over him, turn the lights off in that half of the room and signal the other children to be quiet and get on with their work. I believed that it was important that we as a class gave him a sense of safety and security. The other children were very patient and understanding (Elizabeth).

## A time-out policy

It is important to explain why time-out may be necessary to our class; what time-out (time away from others) actually means and what happens *during* time-out. It is best to do this as part of the establishment phase. The class also needs to know why some children might have to go to time-out. The meaning of unfair – and unacceptable – is related to repetition and degree of disruptive, disturbing or aggressive behaviours.

Time-out – like any consequential aspect of discipline – has its least-to-most intrusive options. There are several basic options. These options need to be discussed across the school and particularly at early years level. *Any* of these time-out options need thoughtful and whole-school (and team) discussion – particularly the duty-of-care aspect as when a child leaves the year/subject class for any *out-of-class* time-out.

Careful records and due follow-up processes are also essential for monitoring of any time-out and for assessment of any children with special needs that might necessitate an individual behaviour plan. (See Chapter 6.)

Staged time-out policy (least-to-most intrusive)

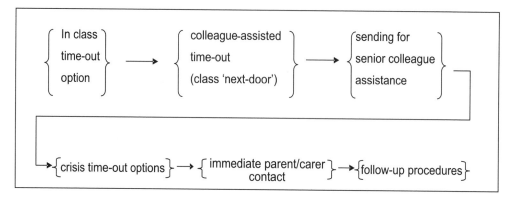

1. *In-class time-out.* We set up an area – in the classroom – (far enough away from the rest of the class proper) so children can have a place to calm down and settle. A small table and chair (no books) and an egg-timer can help.

   Some teachers use a clear bottle filled with water and differently weighted glitter, beads, stones, etc. The child turns it over and watches and waits until everything settles; like an egg timer, but it is calming to watch.

   Some teachers will partly screen the area but the teacher obviously needs to be able to see the child (in terms of duty of care).

   We need to give the time-out 'place' a positive and purposeful name, e.g.: 'cool-off-time area' (see p. 102). Five minutes is – normally – ample for a child to calm, settle and refocus. If the child does not settle and calm down (or does not seem able to) we need to use alternative time-out measures (see below). It is also helpful to give the child a 'cue' whereby they can signal to their teacher they are calm, and settled enough to rejoin their table groups.

   A child's relaxed (non-scowling) arms folded is a helpful (natural) cue. Having escorted a child to time-out the teacher quietly models the 'folded arms', adding: "This will let me know you feel ready to come back to your place and work with your classmates."

   It can also help to have a small poster (laminated) that the child can access in the time-out area. A poster that illustrates a child thinking, calming and realising what he needs to do before he goes back to his table group.

2. *Colleague-assisted time-out.* Many teachers (as noted earlier) are able to cue a colleague in a class next-door (or nearby) with a cue-card or phone call (p. 95). The child would be sent to that class for 15–20 minutes (or sometimes for the rest of that class period). In the other class the child is directed to 'calm and settle', and when the teacher thinks the child is 'ready' they will send him back to his year class (escorted by a trusted child from the support class). It can help

(on some occasions) to give the child some class-work to do (in the other class) if they are settled enough and if (say) there are only 10 or 15 minutes until a recess break.

The important point to remember is that the support colleague does not 'counsel', or give undue special attention, to the child in time-out in their class. Time-out, in this context, is time *away* from the child's 'home' class. It is essential that the child's grade teacher does not 'vilify' the child (who has been directed to leave the class) by saying to her class, "Well I'm glad none of *you* are like Nathan ... his behaviour is terrible isn't it!? Do you know what's going to happen to him? – well it serves him right ...!" This is unnecessary. It is enough to calm, settle, and refocus the class. It is enough to say, 'Nathan will be with Mr/Ms ... for time-out. I'll be speaking with Nathan later. Let's get back to work everyone ..."

3. If a child is significantly disturbing in their disruptive behaviour, or if there is a concern over physical (or psychological) safety, a senior teacher should be sent for (by phone, or cue-card).

The senior teacher (deputy or principal) will then *calmly* escort the disruptive child away from their peer audience.

It is important that the senior colleague not make a fuss by loud-voicing; shouting or threatening – or using hostile body language. A clear, firm, calm voice is normally enough: "Travis ( ... ) come with me. *Now.*" It can sometimes help to verbally cue the child (as above) and walk to the door *as if* the child should follow.

4. *Refusal by a child to leave the class for time-out.* There are occasions where a very disruptive/angry child refuses to leave a classroom for a deputy principal (or even a principal!) On these occasions it is crucial that the senior colleague does not start a huge win/lose fracas (shouting, threatening or dragging the child away). If we cannot enable a child to leave a classroom for necessary time-out (direct him away from the attentional audience of peers) we will need to *direct the audience of peers away* from the very disruptive child. In this case the senior teacher stays with the disruptive child, *in the host class*, while the class teacher escorts the rest of the class away to a place where they can settle and refocus. The disruptive child will often settle down (now that his peer audience has left); enough for the senior teacher to escort him away for supervised time-out.

In a class where I was mentor-teaching my colleague (and I) had had several 'run-ins' with a very challenging young lad. Nathan (age 7) had refused to leave the classroom for time-out. He had persistently disrupted others and was (now) hiding under the computer table loudly muttering swear words, and threats and incantations at me (and several other children). I walked across to my colleague and asked her to take the whole class out calmly, quietly, without loud drama (table group by table group). I would stay and supervise Nathan. He was still swearing as they left.

I tactically ignored him for a few minutes; he eventually stopped swearing and started crying. Later Heather (my colleague) described him as a 'very damaged child' but admitted she had probably given him 'too much rope' early in the year. The next day we set up a personal behaviour recovery programme for Nathan (Chapter 6).

## Parent/carer-contact option

On some occasions it will be necessary to build a parental/carer-contact option into the time-out process. If behaviour is very dangerous, or extreme (or both), it will be necessary to send for the parent/care-giver. Sometimes this option is also built into personal behaviour programmes with very challenging children. It is not always easy to gain co-operation from parent(s)/carers for this 'option'. It is also problematic to engage such an option with unsupportive and challenging parent(s)/carers. Naturally some parent(s)/carers are busy during the day – but this necessary option has to be canvassed with parent(s)/carers whose children present with extreme, challenging, behaviours.

## NB Restraint

There are occasions when a child needs to be physically restrained – for their own safety or for those directly affected by a child's extreme/out-of-control behaviour/aggressive or dangerous behaviour.

- Safety is paramount (for the child, for the class group *and* the teacher).
- *Always* send for a senior teacher (as well as exercising any necessary restraint). Restraint practice should be a whole-school policy and not left to the vagaries of the 'emotional moment' or 'individual interpretation' (Rogers, 2006a).
- Where possible, cue the child verbally before exercising any physical restraint. On some occasions restraint may be as basic as a 'blocking' or restraining hand on a child's hand (or between two children who are in conflict).
- If we need to 'hold' a child (avoid flashing teeth!) it helps to hold from the back (or side, rather from the front) as well as across the chest (watch out for flailing legs!)
- The holding should be firm *but calm*. Always reassure the child we will 'let go of him' when he stops 'kicking and screaming' … or 'trying to jump out/at …' The releasing and relaxing of any physical restraint should be commensurate with the child physically calming themselves. Our calm, clear and 'slower' voice (and word usage) will help here.
- If outside (in the playground), there will be a peer audience; it will help to direct them clearly, firmly, to 'go off and play …'. Children observing (and audience to) high-level conflict (such as a fight) often want 'social permission' to leave – particularly older, 'tougher', 9–11-year-old lads.
- Always write up the restraint incident; *carefully*: the predisposing factors, the participant child(ren), the teacher's restraint behaviours, how the incident progressed and its eventual outcome.
- As with any serious behaviour consequence there should always be senior teacher follow-up support with the teacher, the child and (later) the parent(s)/carer.
- Parent(s)/carers *should* always be notified of any restraint procedures exercised by a teacher in the course of a critical incident.
- Professional development in the area of appropriate safety restraint is available. There are a number of professional development bodies who work with schools in this area and it can help to build this professional knowledge (and skill) into our overall discipline practice. This, of course, will be more relevant in schools who work with high numbers of challenging children.

## 'Safe touch'

With early years children it seems natural to human and relational sensibility to extend an affirming pat on a child's arm. There are many contexts where female teachers will pat a child on the shoulder, put an arm around a child to 'bond', and assure (when they are upset or distressed). Female teachers are frequently seen holding children's hands in playground contexts, or when on out-of-school excursions. This seems relationally normal. Even when we are giving low-intrusive corrective reminders or directions to children, the appropriate use of touch can convey *both* assurance and expectation.

Two children are engaged in overly vigorous conversation during on-task learning time to the extent that no on-task learning is engaged. The teacher comes over to their table and has a quiet reminder ... "Shannon ( ... ) Gary ( ... ) you're having a very loud chat here. Remember, it's class time. Remember, too, your partner-voices ( ... ). What should you be doing with your work now?" Thus she gives a brief reminder and a task-focused question. As she moves away to give them take-up-time she gives a light, affirming pat on each child's arm, *as if to say* "and I know you'll do it ..."

In a UK study addressing 'praise' and 'touch', Wheldhall et al. (1992: 57–9) noted that in classes where teachers gave an 'affirming touch' 'together with praise' that 'on-task behaviour' rose by over 15 per cent and 'disruptive behaviour' fell by about 10 per cent.

It needs to be added – of course – that any such use of 'contingent touch' will only have any positive effect if it is expressed within the overall use of positive behaviour management and encouragement, and if the teacher has a positive working relationship with their children (Rogers, 2006a).

## Male teachers and the way they relate physically to young children

In the current public consciousness *any* such use of 'touch', or an affirming pat on the arm, or an arm around the shoulders ... needs collegial consideration. What is appropriate? What do we mean by *appropriate*? Normally we would not need to ask that question; common sense, professionalism, decency and emotional intelligence ought to be adequate. As teachers we have a significant duty-of-care role (for a third of a child's waking day) and we stand as *noblesse oblige* in relation to children.

In 'today's climate' some parents/carers will register concern about the normal, tactile behaviour of teachers – most particularly male teachers. While most early years teachers are female, there are many subject teachers who are male (and, of course, senior male staff).

It is unfortunate that when a male teacher 'touches' a child (in a normal, affirming way) that it can be seen as – perhaps – 'ethically ambiguous' in a way it would not be with a female teacher. Females are traditionally (in all cultures) seen as nurturing, caring, protective. Most males, too, are (naturally) nurturing, caring, and protective, but in the 'public context' of education – and the care-giving aspect of a teacher's role these days – the male teacher has to have a heightened consciousness regarding how they relate physically to young children.

- Touch on the upper arm (no arms around waist, or drawing a child closer with arm around the waist, no sitting of child on the lap). One can image a parent seeing a child sitting on a male teacher's lap as 'significantly different' from a child sitting on a female teacher's lap.
- If a child is distressed, while giving obvious verbal assurance – and calming – it will help to have a female teacher present to extend any 'physical reassurance'.
- In any one-to-one chat with a child (p. 87f) – with both female child and male teacher – leave the classroom door open. In any *extended* one-to-one chat, or behaviour interview of a male teacher with a *female* child, it will help to have a female colleague present. She does not need to be 'involved' in the interview necessarily – but it is helpful if she is *there*, abstractedly doing her work programme (whatever).

It seems annoyingly cautious (and I hope not professionally patronising to my male colleagues!) that I have spent a little time on this topic. It only takes a few unthinkably swinish, evil, men in our profession to cast the public slur on all male teachers. (Bill)

There is television exposure (as there should be) each year, detailing the rare – but horrific – cases.

Children need positive, affirming, caring, morally strong, male role-models in their lives. Schooling forms a critically important part of a child's life and their development. It would be very sad if the right males self-exclude from our profession because of fear of social taint simply because they are *male* teachers.

## Time-out is not a last resort

It is distressing – very distressing – to see a teacher loudly shouting (even screaming) at a child whose behaviour has 'pushed them to their limit ...'. Time-out should not be seen as the *last possible resort*. On some occasions time-out will need to be the first response/consequence; as when a significant safety issue is at stake, or when the child has been disturbingly violent, or has 'lost' any sense of self-control.

Some teachers may be concerned that they will be seen as 'weak', 'ineffective' or that they 'can't cope' if they utilise out-of-class time-out options. Time-out procedures are there for a reason. If a teacher is 'over-using' this consequential step that will be a signal for senior staff to offer constructive support rather than blame.

## 'Plea bargaining'

It is pointless to argue with a child; to 'plead', 'negotiate' or 'bargain' in any context where time-out is a necessity – "You promise me you'll be a good boy now?" Of course they will, "I'll be good forever!" "I won't do it again!"

If we have said to a child, "If you continue to … (be brief and specific, about their unacceptable behaviour) you'll have to go to time-out", it is crucial we carry this consequence through. All the children (not just the child directed to time-out) need to see the calm, fair, 'justice' of any time-out consequence by a teacher.

My colleague and I were working with our class of 6–7-year-olds on a 'recipe book' (this was to be used later in some simple in-class 'cooking', see below). It was on-task learning time and a co-operative learning activity.

As my colleague and I moved around to each table – kneeling down at eye-level – (I cannot crouch any more at 60 years of age; it's a one knee-bend these days!). We encouraged, clarified, gave feedback …

I noticed, out of the corner of my eye, that Damien was annoying Matthew with a felt-tipped pen ('pretending' to draw on his work). Matthew told him to stop it. I then heard a yell, turned and saw Damien 'stab' Matthew several times on the arm with the felt-tipped pen.

I called him over for cool-off-time. "Damien ( … ) Damien ( … ). Pen down and over here. Time-out." He protested and started to 'plea bargain', "I'll be alright Mr Rogers, I'm sorry!!" I repeated the direction to 'come with me for cool-off-time'.

I walked across to the cool-off-time area, Damien followed, frowning and stamping his feet. I directed him to sit, and calm down. Damien sat – and sulked – in the time-out area for 5 minutes or so. I asked another table group if Damien could work at their table until the end of that lesson. (I did not want Damien sitting next to Matthew for the rest of the day.) They were very accommodating (as children so often are).

Later that day, at lunchtime, I directed Damien to stay back and we worked through several questions to enable him to focus on his behaviour. The outcome of this after-class chat was a private apology to Matthew. He wrote it out and – later – gave it to Matthew with a verbal apology. Matthew's response was, "That's OK", he even smiled at Damien. It is amazing what some children will put up with.

Turning to Damien I said, "It's not alright when anyone in our class hits, pokes, pushes or punches ..." "Matthew do you mean it's OK, like it's over now? What did you mean when you said it's OK?" I was reassuring with Matthew. I was sure he had meant, "It's OK *now* that Damien's sorry ...". He explained that things were alright now that Damien had said sorry and that he said he wouldn't do anything like that again.

As a further consequence, for the rest of the day, Damien worked at a different table group.

We *always* distinguish between tiredness, 'silly' behaviour and *repeatedly* distracting behaviours, or potentially dangerous behaviours or a single act of dangerous or violent behaviour. Time-out is not *merely* a punishment; it enables a demonstrable – and fair – calming behaviour consequence.

## Key questions for a 'time-out plan'

- What sorts of behaviours would we normally utilise *in-class* time-out for?
- What sorts of behaviours/situations would we normally exercise *out-of-class* time-out for?

- How will we explain the concept of time-out to our children?
- What *term* shall we adopt for our classroom (or early years department) when expressing the concept and purpose of time-out?
- What sorts of things might we say when framing a direction to a child to 'go to the time-out area ...' for aggressive, violent, behaviours?
- What should we do if a child flatly refuses to go to the time-out area? – or refuses out-of-class time-out?
- What is our early years department back-up support plan? Any early years plan should also be consistent with whole-school behaviour policy.
- At what point are parent(s)/carers notified?
- If a child has been in time-out several times (in close succession over – say – several days) what is our preferred next step?

## Terminology

Terminology is important for the concept and practice of time-out with children. 'Cool-off time' and 'thinking time' are common examples of usage. We have heard typical (and unacceptable) terms such as 'naughty-corner', or 'naughty-chair'. The worst terms we have ever heard are 'sin-bin' and 'shame table' (both bad theology and bad psychology). The key emphasis in the use of time-out as a behaviour consequence is to link the relatedness of any *repeated* distracting (or unsafe or dangerous) behaviour with time-*out*, or time-*away, from the group.*

Children should know – in the establishment phase of the year – that if they 'make it difficult' for other children to learn (give several common examples) then they will be asked to work away from other children; or sit in cool-off time *away* from other children. This means that 'you will not be allowed to sit with other children. You will have to calm down and think about your behaviour: what you did that was wrong and what you can do to make things better'. It is important we explain what 'calming down' means.

When I was pregnant with my first child, a boy was transferred to our school and was put into my class later in the term. To date, he is the most difficult child I have ever dealt with. He would not stay on task, would ignore any instruction, would run away from school (out of the gates) to get attention. He physically pulled me over on several occasions. When his behaviour started to become a danger to me (and I was too 'fat' to run after him), I was lucky enough to have the support of Dianne, the teacher in the classroom next door. I should add here that our school had a policy of allowing children to address all teachers by their first name. This is not a common practice in Australian schools but I soon got used to it; it certainly did not present the concerns I initially imagined.

On one particular day when Shane was wreaking havoc, I put in place the new warning system. "If you don't do what I'm asking, I'll have to take you next door to Di." Much to my frustration, he bolted, out of the classroom, out of the gates and down the street. I stuck my head in next door (Dianne's class), "Shane's done a runner again!" So Di sent a couple of her 11-year-olds to coax him back; he was still in view of our classrooms. When he finally returned, Di took him to the staffroom, sat him down and asked him what the problem was. Di popped her head into my room and called me over, in a hushed voice she said to me, "He said you told him you were going to kill him; you wouldn't say anything like that …?" "No, of course not" I replied, "I just gave him a warning and said I'd 'send him next door to Di'." We looked at each other as the penny dropped. Her name was Di; he actually thought he was going next door to 'die'. I went to the staffroom and sat him on my lap and explained that her name was Dianne and we called her Di for short. We gave each other a cuddle and all had a giggle about it.

## Going to the principal's office[22]

Gone (one hopes) are the days when some teachers would send a child to the principal to get 'bawled out'. The child then (some teachers hope) will come back verbally chastised, and chastened, never to do "'x', 'y', 'z' again". This creates unnecessary anxiety in all children about 'going to the principal's office'. Going to the principal's office should – normally – be a pleasant experience: teachers will send children to share their work; a child 'delegation' to share a class concern (this should be prefaced by an appointment); receiving a 'special sticker' for work or social service …

What is disconcerting is when children who are frequently disruptive are given 'child of the week' certificates for minimal effort or as a 'reward' for hopeful future behaviour. This is unfair to the majority of children who work solidly and consistently and gives a false 'social' kudos to the child concerned. Further, it is not the principal's job to punish the child *at the point of time-out support*; their task (at this juncture) is to give the year/subject teacher immediate – unquestioned – time-out support.

It is advisable that the principal does not set up any counselling for the child *at the point of time-out*. It also does not help things if the principal gives the child a special 'job'; "Would you like to do a special job for Mrs Smith?" Some children may associate their disruptive behaviour with a positive time-out experience and (consequentially) mis-cue why they are in time-out. Counselling *and* 'special privileges' are (of course) totally appropriate supports for children, but unhelpful when associated with time-out.

Any follow-up 'secondary' consequences (following the primary consequence of time-out) should always be developed by the year/subject teacher – with *support* from the senior teachers or principal. For example: completing set class work or engaging children in restitution.

## Rotation of (the) child

Sounds a trifle unusual?

Sometimes teachers who teach, work with and support *very* challenging children need a break. 'Classroom rotation' involves sending such children to another classroom – for a full class period to give the class teacher such a relieving 'break'.

Once, even twice a week, the most demanding children are sent to another class (either with set work, or work is provided by the class teacher of the 'support class'). This – effectively – gives the teacher, and the class, a 'break' from the distracting and disruptive behaviour of the child in question.

It needs to be stressed – however – that this option is not to be confused with time-out. Its primary purpose is to give the class teacher (and her class) 'a relieving break'. It needs to be exercised collegially and supportively and always balanced with the personal behaviour programme approach noted in Chapter 6.

### Exclusion from *social* play

Evan (almost 7 years old) had been reported several times for throwing wood chips (and sand on several occasions) at other children. He had also used sticks to threaten, throw at, or hit, other children.

While he had faced several time-out sessions (at play time) his teacher (in consultation with her senior colleagues) decided on a twofold strategy that it was hoped would balance necessary and appropriate consequences on the one hand, while supporting and protecting the safety of other children on the other.

It is important to stress that the class teacher had spoken with the child several times about his behaviour (beyond time-out). She had also encouraged – and initiated – restitution through apologies (not always given). She had also tried talking it through with his mother – with mixed success.

For a period of one week Evan had no *social* play; this was a key element in his social-behavioural consequence. It was explained to him that, "If you keep hurting other children by throwing sand at them, and hitting them with sticks, then you won't be able to play with other children. We can't let you hurt other children by ..." (The class teacher specifically outlined his hurtful behaviours ...). "You will have a play time, but you won't be playing *with* other children; you'll have your playtime *by yourself* while the other children in class are doing their classwork ..."

He protested and tried to bargain. "No! Miss – I'll be good. I won't chuck any sticks ...! I won't!!" His teacher assured him: "I know you're upset. I can see you're upset about this but we can't let you keep hurting children. So, this week you have your play times by yourself, with a teacher looking after you ..."

It was difficult (labour intensive) to set up this roster for individualised play supervision, but it was an effective lesson in *social* consequences for Evan.

His 'play area' was located where other children (in class time) could not see him. He was closely supervised for his 'play time'; he frequently sulked and complained it was 'all unfair'. He was *briefly* reminded why his play time would 'have to be like this'. It was essential, too, for his teachers to communicate with him at all times in a respectful calm way; at times firm – but always respectful. It was also important not to pity Evan or excuse his previous hostile and aggressive behaviour.

The mother was 'in favour' of this approach (in preference to 'keeping him home from school for a few days suspension ...'). We were patiently careful to emphasise we were not merely punishing him but trying to teach him the link between social play, safety and how to treat others.

The school believed it had given Evan significant 'chances' and 'options'. It was hoped that this *experiental* consequence would enable him to understand the link between his behaviour and his – temporary – exclusion from *social* play.

The second emphasis, in this process, was to work one-to-one with Evan on social play behaviours. These sessions were conducted during lunch play times. A room was made available and there two teachers worked on a play-skills programme with Evan (and several other boys) during their 'time-in'. There was some brief counselling, and role-play, but the emphasis was always on teaching simple strategies for *social* play.

After that week, Evan was allowed his normal play times. He was well aware – by now – of the consequences of hurting others. There were lapses, but there was significant improvement in his playground behaviour and his general attitude to other children. All the teachers on playground duty were made aware of Evan's 'programme' and why it had been instituted. Any consequence that modifies – or deprives – a child (temporarily) of social play needs careful collegial consideration and parent/carer support if the consequential aim is to be realised.

## Bullying

Bullying is a behaviour that *intends* to hurt others. It is selective, intentional and purposeful. Unlike those reactive hits, spits or punches, bullying occurs when the perpetrator (even at 5 years of age) senses, feels, begins to 'know' that they have relational and social power yet uses this 'power' to hurt others psychologically or physically. Bullies rarely bully alone; they need the social (peer) attentional 'acceptance' or 'approval' to confirm their bullying behaviour. This 'social' collusion makes bullying an extremely disturbing pattern of behaviour. It should never be tolerated, excused or minimised.

Most bullying is psychological; *repeated* taunts, teasing, name-calling, friendship exclusion. Most bullying occurs in non-classroom settings; this makes our need for vigilant awareness even more important. It behoves teachers to be vigilant if they sense, or suspect, any child to be a victim of bullying behaviour.

Classroom discussions are a crucial forum for raising group awareness of bullying behaviour. At such classroom meetings teachers will enable group awareness by asking questions such as:

- '*What* does bullying behaviour *look* like ...?', '*sound like* ...?', '*feel* like ...?'
- We also ask, '*why* do some people bully others?' (give some common examples).
- 'What should we do when we see someone who is being bullied'? (give examples)

It is not uncommon for children who witness bullying behaviour (at the actual time it occurs) not to get involved. This is perhaps an understandable human trait ('fear', 'confusion', 'uncertainty'). In class discussions we need to address this issue and distinguish between reporting and telling tales. 'Telling tales' is often trying to get someone into trouble. Reporting is letting an adult know what is going on about the bullying behaviour (or any significantly disturbing behaviours) so adults can help make it stop and help and support those being hurt.

It is important to clarify children's understandings about bullying behaviour. The ill-thought reactive push or shove, the silly play fighting, the 'dropped' swear word, the use of words like 'silly' or 'stupid' are not behaviours – in themselves – that constitute bullying. While any such behaviour needs to be addressed with normal discipline (and necessary consequences) it is the *selective and repetitive intent* that we normally associate with *bullying behaviour*. Sometimes a parent or carer will say their child was bullied because someone tripped them over, or said they were stupid or an idiot ... We need to be careful in what we *mean*, and address, as *bullying behaviour*. Tripping someone up is wrong (and should be addressed) but is not, of itself, necessarily bullying.

One of the most helpful picture story books we have found for raising awareness in early years about bullying is the book *No More Bullying!* by Rosemary Stones. It outlines a friendship exclusion incident (with a girl) and how the victim feels in (and out of) school and how it affects the behaviour of the victim, the bully and the peer audience. It also discusses how such behaviour can be mis-cued, and how it can be *thoughtfully* addressed. It is particularly helpful in illustrating how schools – and parents/carers – can work together to address bullying.

It is a book that also addresses the ambiguities that can surround bullying behaviour at this age.

## Restitution

Restitution is – basically – 'putting things right'; or as right as can be. It involves reparation, repairing and rebuilding in word or deed (from the Latin verb 'to set up').

## Case study

Sean (aged 6) had kicked Danielle's paper carrier bag of Barbie (and 'Cindy' and 'Vicky' dolls). He had split the bag open; the contents spilling on the path. He though it was 'fun', and he was '*just* mucking around'; it had got 'out of hand'.

It happened just before classroom entry (entrails of play time). I had seen this happen through the window. As Danielle came in (clutching the dolls and split bag) she was crying. I reassured Danielle; we put the dolls/bag next to the teacher's desk for the time being. I asked her if she would stay back at lunchtime to tell Sean what she felt about all this and what he could do to help "fix things".

I had already discussed understandings of restitution with the whole class. I told Sean he would have to stay back after class (at lunchtime) to explain what he had done to Danielle. He started to protest ('I was just ...'). I directed him to the mat; it was whole-class teaching time. I had seen the whole episode. Later (at lunchtime) I directed Sean and Danielle to stay back.

They sat facing each other. I asked Danielle to explain what had happened and how she felt about what Sean had done and what she wanted to happen – from Sean and from my support as (a) teacher. She wanted him to say sorry and *not* do anything like that again.

When it was Sean's turn he quickly apologised and said 'he was only joking'. I explained *any* kicking of *anyone's* property was *never joking* (and briefly explained why).

He immediately apologised. I asked him what he could do to help fix things. He looked puzzled at first and then offered to fix (up) the bag. I asked how and he (surprisingly) mentioned the 'special book-tape' (very strong bookbinding tape he had seen).

He stayed in at playtime and spent a good 15 minutes – with a bit of help – taping up the bag. Later I called Danielle and Sean together and he (sheepishly) presented the bag with a second apology which she (sheepishly) accepted.

- Two (6-year-old) lads who had trampled over new seedlings planted by the groundsman helped him, later (beyond their apology), to replant new ones.
- Children who damage *any* property are required to undertake 'time-trade tasks' (as a civic restitution) to help 'repay' damage (through their time). See appendix C.

■ Children write, or draw, apology statements (at a calmer time) and exercise their apology with teacher support. They, obviously, do this at a calmer time; one-to-one with their teacher. A student who has accepted an apology is encouraged to respond and also ask for reassurance this (their behaviour) will not happen again.

■ In a bullying issue, restitution is not always an easy possibility. To enable any *emotional* restitution the victim must be allowed to confront the bully (with teacher support) at a planned one-to-one meeting. The victim of such bullying plans – with their class teacher – how they will make clear to the bully what it is they did or said (or have been doing or saying); how they (the victim) feel about this bullying behaviour – and how it has affected them; what they want the bullying child to do about this and to give reassurance the bullying behaviour will stop. This can be a very powerful, and emotionally reassuring step, for a victim of bullying:

– It exposes the previous 'secrecy' the bully had from teachers knowing about their bullying.
– The victim has the opportunity to say what they want (and often need) to say.
– It is always advisable to plan ahead, with the victim of the bullying, the sorts of things they want to say.
– Such meetings should always be elective for the victim; we should encourage, never force, such opportunities.

In any such accountability meeting (Rogers, 2006a) it is essential to have a review meeting with both children in a few days, or a week's time "to see how things are going in the playground …".[23] This in part reassures the victim, it also lets the perpetrator know we will track/monitor/review their behaviour.

Children's emotional, psychological and physical safety is paramount at school. We need to take all bullying (harassing) behaviour seriously and support the victim initially but also give them a supported voice in 'confronting' the bully about their behaviour/s. We then need to monitor, and review, the bully's ongoing behaviour in respect of the victim.

# Chapter 6

## Children with social, emotional and behavioural difficulties

### Challenging child behaviours and children with social, emotional and behavioural difficulties

### What can we control in a child's behaviour?

Children who display frequent and durable patterns of disruptive behaviour some-times have a complex and stressful 'causative pathology' affecting their school behaviour and learning at school. We obviously cannot control significant family dysfunction; we cannot control long-term unemployment or structural poverty or substance abuse; we cannot control the kind of (and amount of) television some young children watch and we cannot control their diet at home.[24]

While we can, and must, utilise due process for children at risk from disturbing and, even, dangerous causative pathologies (from some home environments), we should not re-victimise the child *while he is with us at school*. When we – effec-tively – say 'a child cannot help his behaviour because he has a single mother, and she is living with an unsupportive male "care-giver" (to put it 'kindly') and he is unemployed, *and* the television is always on, *and* there are several children by sev-eral fathers, *and* there is substance abuse, *and* ...', we – effectively – say he is an inevitable victim of such 'causitive pathology' (Rogers, 2003a).[25] How on earth can we 'control' all *that*? While teachers are almost universally empathetic about the tragic needs of some children, it is important we do not *treat* the child as a 'victim' while he is with us at school. Teacher 'victimising' of a child, *because* of their home environment, often means treating them in a way that makes them stand out from other children. It may also appear to other children that we are **109** 'excusing' behaviour we would never accept in other children.

When we excuse a child's behaviour because of 'causative pathology' we effectively say 'you can't really help your behaviour here'. We also effectively say 'we can't really help you either'. That is both unfair and unhelpful (for the child as well as his classmates who witness the child's aberrant and disruptive behaviour).

Behaviour is not only *conditioned* by factors outside of the school environment, behaviour is also *learned* – in context. We need to use the third of a child's waking day – while they are with us – to enable him to develop more effective, and helpful, behaviour choices.

Many early years colleagues – over the years – have said to us that *for some children* school is the safest, sanest, place in their lives. A place where new, and positive, learnings about self and others can take place.

"Creeping like snail (un)*willingly* to school ..." Shakespeare (slightly adapted from As You Like It, Act 2: 7).

## Behaviour recovery

There is a small percentage (perhaps an increasing percentage) of children in our schools who have been diagnosed with behaviour disorders. Behaviour disorders range across a spectrum within which the features of such behaviour are displayed. The frequency, durability and intensity of, say, outbursts from children with Attention Deficit Disorder (ADD) are familiar to many teachers.

At the 'lower' end of such a 'spectrum' children (mostly boys) would display apparent difficulty in concentration, focus, attention and displays of kinaesthetic restlessness often characterised by teachers as *overly* active or *hyper*active.

Further along the spectrum there are those children with diagnosed ADHD (attention deficit hyperactivity disorder) who can (and often do) benefit from clinical diagnosis and medication. At the more extreme end of the ADD spectrum is there every second rugby and football player?

Whether the behaviour disorder is professionally diagnosed or not (say in autistic spectrum behaviour such as Asperger's syndrome; or Tourette's syndrome; or Oppositional Defiance Disorder …) disordered *behaviour* is present; that is the hard reality teachers have to work with.

When there is high frequency – and durability – of disruptive behaviours across a range of classroom settings it is crucial that teachers work together to support the child 'at risk'. We also need to consciously address the wider rights of the other children affected by such behaviours and of the teachers who work with these children and of the parent(s)/carer(s) of the child 'at risk.

## Attentional behaviour

There are children who have learned that if they badger an adult ('Mum, mum, mum!'; becoming – at school – 'Miss, Miss, Miss …!') then their need for attention will be met. Some children will hit out at a sibling, or snatch a sibling's favourite toy, to (seemingly?) create the resultant attentional fracas. Even if the parental attention is 'negative' in expression – they are *noticed* and attended to. Some children have learned to wave 'the attentional flag' early – perhaps because of sibling placement; differential sibling approval by parent(s)/carers; behaviour disorders (such as attention deficit hyperactivity disorder). Children bring these attentional behaviour patterns to school as they test out their need to 'belong'.

The need for attention ('I am noticed') is a fundamental need in human beings (at any age). The kind of, and degree of, attention one 'needs' and the amount of attention will vary according to one's experience, upbringing and sense of emotional security. (Witness the rise of television 'reality' shows.)

Some children come from homes where they have had to 'fight' for any parental attention – in large families, or where the parental/care-giver upbringing in terms of discipline and any encouragement is characteristically negative.

Some children will compensate for insecurity about their sense of worth and how they conceive that worth (in a relational or social sense) by drawing significant attention to themselves. Some children will do this in overt ways: clowning, silly comments or noises, hiding under tables … other children draw attention to themselves in repeatedly, and *overly*, 'nice' or 'acceptable' ways. Most of us have worked with children who use characteristic expressive 'cuteness' to draw attention to themselves. The child who comes up to the busy teacher (in on-task learning time) and says, "Can you see my writing Miss?", with an overly cute facial expression. The teacher acknowledges their work. The same child then proceeds to come back to the teacher again, and again, and again – with the same overt cuteness and voice, "Did I do a nice coloured border Miss …?", "Did I write neat?", "Do you like it Miss?", "Is it good work?" I have had colleagues say, "I feel like saying, "If you come over to me *one more time* and ask me if your work is 'good' or 'nice' I'll …!"

It is as if the child only feels significant (in the classroom setting) if the teacher *frequently* notices, attends, assures and overservices the child's attentional needs.

## Goal and behaviour

These behaviours are often the child's way of saying 'NOTICE ME!'; they are – in a sense – their 'goal' (even if such a goal is not fully conscious to the child). The child who repeatedly calls out (during whole-class teaching time); who frequently calls out before others (and does not have anything to say or, if they do, it is something annoyingly irrelevant); the child who constantly annoys others to get a reaction … Attentional behaviour is the bane and normative challenge of a teacher's life.

Children who are (fortunately) secure in their sense of self do not need to seek attention in these overt ways. Their attentional needs – in the schooling context – are met through socially co-operative means.

The kinds of negative attentional behaviours, or attentional power-seeking behaviours, can also be significantly affected by the kinds of peer – and adult – attention they receive. Difficult as it is, reactive, or 'overservicing', responses by teachers to attentional behaviours, often reinforce the very behaviour we are seeking to help the child modify. While it is easy to say this in print, it is a very difficult exercise in the busy day-to-day practice of the classroom.

We should never *simply* ignore extreme attentional behaviour, as if by such ignoring such behaviour will then not be reinforced and will go away. 'Ignoring' of *some* aspects of attentional, or attentional-deficit behaviour, should always be *tactical* ignoring (p. 62f). Even *tactical* ignoring is a context-dependent teacher skill that needs to be combined with clear, calm, firm use of directional language (p. 55), choice-consequence language (p. 56) and deferred (or immediate) behaviour consequences (p. 73).

It is also crucial to follow-up any persistent attentional behaviours – beyond classroom time – even on day one (p. 87f). Where early follow-up and follow-through do not occasion any change in such attentional behaviours it will often help if the class teacher works on an individual behaviour management plan with the child (see below).

## Behaviour recovery: teaching children through individual behaviour plans

Jackson was frequently calling out during whole-class teaching time. His calling out was mostly attentionally silly comments. He would also make silly faces at the other children. This behaviour occurred almost every time the children sat together on the carpet area for whole-class teaching time. The teacher frequently directed him to put his hand up, to keep his hands safe, to listen ... He would stop his attentional behaviour for a while and start again.

If you could watch from the side (as I did) you could sense his attentional need expressed in his behaviour: "notice ME!" Some children laughed, some were annoyed, some told him to stop it, thus creating more attentional focus and peer friction.

My colleague had – obviously – spoken with him after class. On several occasions he had to be sent to time-out (both in and out of class). The principal had spoken with him (several times).

This is a frustratingly common scenario. I was there.

Jackson's behaviour can be considered disordered because of its frequency, durability (the behaviour is more than 'bad-day syndrome') and generality (he also behaved that way in specialist classes).Up to 5 per cent of children in Australian schools are considered to be 'behaviourally disordered' (Rogers, 2003a).

## Behaviour recovery

Children like Jackson will very often benefit from an *individual behaviour plan* that emphasises, and teaches, the necessary skills to enable classroom learning and socialisation. Some children need some *individual* teaching time to learn 'basic' (but essential) behaviour skills such as: *how* to sit on the mat; *how* to listen; *how* to ask questions; *how* to seek teacher help (in whole-class, and on-task, learning time); *how* to wait their turn; *how* to sit and work at their table groups ...

Even *how* to line up and enter a classroom (without annoying others) is a basic social skill that some children need to be taught *one to one*.

It is commonplace for teachers to say, "But these children should know how to 'line-up' by now, how to sit on the mat, and raise their hand, and use reasonable voice levels ..." – that is true in one sense. Most early years teachers spend focused time in the establishment phase of the year explaining, discussing and role-playing behaviours that are essential to classroom life. A small percentage of children will still need one-to-one attention – with their class teacher – to focus on, and practise, and consolidate those skills. It is our belief that those children have a 'behaviour need' as acute as any learning need (O'Brien, 1999; Rogers, 1998; 2003a).

We do not hide from the fact that these children may have very troubled lives *outside of school* (p. 109f). 'At risk' children will often need specialist help (through counselling and family welfare support). They will still need the 'academic survival skills', and 'social survival skills', essential *in a school context* for the third of the day they are with us. In this sense learning is not merely conditioned it is also context-dependant.

The Behaviour Recovery model is an educational model; it emphasises the teaching of essential social and learning skills that the child needs at school. The Behaviour Recovery programme is developed within a one-to-one teaching context. In this setting the *class teacher* will identify the child's behaviour skill needs through picture cues and role modelling, and then use rehearsal skills, practising and regular ongoing feedback to clarify and consolidate desired behaviour.

## Step 1 *The behaviour profile*

The key questions we ask revolve around the behaviour of at-risk children in the first one to two weeks of the first term:

- How *frequent* is the distracting, or disruptive, behaviour?
- How *durable* is the distracting, or disruptive, behaviour? Is it several times, in *every* lesson, of *every* day? (i.e.: more than 'bad-day syndrome'?)
- How *general* is the distracting, disruptive, behaviour? (Is the *frequent* and *durable* pattern of behaviour typically occurring across classes other than the grade teacher's class?)

It is essential that there is a whole-school approach to working with such at-risk children and whole-school colleague support in establishing and maintaining any individual behaviour plans. This is particularly acute when utilising time-out options. It is also essential that colleagues have a supportive, no-blame, collegiality when working with challenging children. It is taxing and demanding on a teacher's professional and personal goodwill when they give of their non-contact time to develop individual behaviour support programmes for these children. It behoves us all to support one another in a shared awareness, understanding and development of such plans, and to always give consistent collegial back-up.

When a child's behaviour presents with a behaviour pattern (within the profile noted above) the class teacher will notify the team leader and administration and set aside one-to-one sessions to teach the child necessary behaviour skills. This one-to-one time is normally allocated to non-contact times (lunchtime) with 15 to 20 minutes for each session.

In larger schools time release for the class teacher (to work with a child one to one) is sometimes an option.

## Step 2 *Identifying the behaviour concerns with the child*

With our colleagues we find it helpful to use the first one-to-one session with the child to focus on their distracting/ disruptive behaviour/s; we do this through visual cueing and *brief* 'behaviour mirroring' (Rogers, 2003a).

We have a prepared drawing of the child that illustrates his distracting/disruptive behaviour (see Fig. 1).

Fig. 1

Simple 'stick figures' illustrate the child, his peers and his class teacher. The faces of the class peers and teacher are shown looking 'sad' (social annoyance and disapproval) – in response to the child's calling out/loudness/pushing/task avoidance (or whatever behaviour we have pictured). This picture cue-card is then used as a means of conversing with the child about his disruptive behaviour. The 'picture cue' enables the child's behaviour awareness as the teacher focuses a conversation around the picture.

The tenor of the conversation with the child needs to be positive, respectful, calm, reassuring and supportive: "Have a look at this picture, who do you think this is?" The teacher points to the child in the illustration; *then* to the teacher and his class peers. Almost all children will immediately nominate themselves as the child calling out (or whatever we have illustrated as his typical disruptive behaviour ...). "What are you doing? – Have a look at the picture." Avoid asking the child '*Why*' he is calling out (or ...). Some children will say they are 'being naughty', or 'silly', or will simply 'describe' what they see. It is important (here) that the teacher focuses on the child's disruptive behaviour, "What are you doing ... (that is 'naughty' or 'silly' ...)?" Some children will say nothing. The teacher will then calmly describe the child's disruptive behaviour as signified in the illustration (e.g. Fig. 1).

It can also help strengthen the child's behaviour awareness by *briefly* mirroring their typical distracting/disruptive behaviour. 'Mirroring' is an activity where the adult role-plays the child's typical disruptive behaviour (p. 90).

My Plan

1. Sit on the mat with safe hands and feet.

2. Put my hand up (without calling out).

3. Think about what I want to say (does it makes sense? does it fit?).

4. Speak clearly.

5. Wait for the teacher to call on me.

Fig. 2

- Always ask the child's permission: "I'd like to show you what it looks like (or sounds like) when you ... (e.g.: call out, annoy others on the mat ...)" or "Do you mind if I show you ...?" Most children will initially be unsure what we mean but respond with a 'yes' or 'OK'.
- When we mirror a child's disruptive behaviour, we do so *briefly* and then step away and sit back down on a chair. The 'stepping away' from the place where

we 'mirror' the child's disruptive behaviour conveys an important psychological message. For example: showing a child how he rolls on the mat and hides under a table during whole-class teaching time; many children will naturally laugh at this (some will laugh with natural anxiety, some because it *looks* funny to see an adult portraying a child …). Our 'stepping away' (from the 'mirrored' behaviour) gives the child the physical reassurance that we are – now – their teacher speaking *about* their behaviour. The behaviour mirroring gives a kind of concrete–operational 'anchor' for the child's awareness and understanding about their behaviour and its effect on others. Not all children like the initial illustration (that pictures the disruptive child), "I don't like that picture!" We reply; "Nor do I; I like *this* picture though. Have a look at *this* …". Here the teacher shows the child the picture that illustrates the child behaving appropriately (see Fig. 2).

NB It is important in any behaviour plan to initially focus on one key pattern of behaviour, e.g.: 'rolling around on the mat, calling out, restlessness etc. … *on the mat*'. The focus behaviour skill is, therefore, 'How to sit on the mat', and why we sit 'this way' (*without* rolling around or calling out).

It can also help to start any 'behaviour recovery' by addressing the most disruptive of behaviours – they (after all) are the most stressful for teacher and the rest of the class.

Behaviour will normally fall into a pattern of attentional, or avoidance behaviours; by breaking down the *appropriate* behaviour pattern into teachable skills we enable the child to experience the self-esteem that comes with peer approval and teacher approval (and, in time, self-approval).

The key to behaviour recovery is clarifying – and actually teaching – the desired behaviour in the one-to-one setting.

## Step 3

The second drawing identifies, and illustrates, the expected (necessary) behaviours (Fig. 2). In this picture the child, teacher and peers have smiles on their faces symbolising social approval. This is an important teaching point. Many of these children do behave attentionally; in self-defeating ways. A crucial feature – in any behaviour recovery – is to build a child's confidence in behaviour that will enable *appropriate* attention and social approval.

Key questions: When talking with the child there are several questions we raise to clarify his understanding about his plan. "What are you doing in this picture?"

Many children will say (as in this example), "I'm sitting on the mat" (see Fig. 2).

"What else are you doing?" A typical answer (with such a plan) is "Listening to my teacher?" – such an answer may be the extent of the child's awareness of their behaviour in the picture. The teacher clarifies and develops the child's behaviour awareness by asking, "What are you doing with your hands?, feet?, voice? … *How* …? *Where* are you sitting …?" Any 'why' questions are utilised to strengthen behaviour importance: "Why is it important to put your hand up *without* calling out or clicking your fingers?" All these questions are helping the child to focus *their* thinking on *their* behaviour.

Children – obviously – like this second picture. It illustrates behaviour 'success' and social acceptance and their teacher, too, is looking happy (less stressed!).

*Any* pattern of behaviour we work on with a child is always referenced back to our classroom behaviour agreement. This 'normalises' the child's expected, targeted, behaviours within the classroom community. (See Chapter 2.)

## Step 4 Modelling

The teacher then models the specific 'target' behaviour pattern as noted in the second picture. In Jackson's case the teacher sat on the mat (the child sat watching) and faced an empty chair and modelled 'how to sit'; how to 'think first before asking a question …'; 'waiting until the teacher chooses …'; 'speaking clearly …'; 'how to listen with eyes and hands'; 'how to put up (their) hand *without* calling out …'. All these elements make up a *pattern* of reasonable 'sitting on the mat and listening and sharing if you want to say something'.

## Step 5

The child practises/rehearses the desired target behaviour and the teacher gives immediate, *brief* (non-judgemental) feedback. This helps clarify and fine-tune the behaviour expectations. The referent 'anchor' is the picture-plan. The teacher will actually nominate the picture as the 'child's plan' (see Fig. 2).

The teacher explains to the child that a copy of 'his plan' will be given to all the teachers (subject teachers) and the principal "… so they can know how they can help you with your plan."

## Parents and carers

Parents or carers are also shown a copy of the plan (at any subsequent parent/carer–teacher meeting about their child's progress …). The teacher will explain the Behaviour Recovery model, emphasising how 'this plan' will help *their* child with *their overall learning* at school.

## Peer-partner

It can often help to have a peer-partner for the child to assist them with their plan in class time. We find it helpful to give the child a 'choice' between two or three responsible children who they might want to help them in classtime to help them remember, and do, their plan. It is essential we check with the suggested peer-partners beforehand and prepare them for the extent (and limits) of their 'peer role'. Their role will be to *quietly* remind (non-verbally at times) and encourage their classmate within the target behaviour expectations.

## Playground

Similar plans – using the Behaviour Recovery model – have been successfully used in non-classroom settings (Rogers, 2003a). The key elements involve identifying the disruptive behaviour and teaching the necessary playground behaviour through picture cueing; mirroring; modelling; rehearsal and peer-partnering. With any individual playground behaviour plans it is essential that *all* teachers, on *any duty*, are aware of which children are on a behaviour plan (for the playground or other non-classroom settings). It will also be important to have a clear time-out plan for hostile, aggressive or running-away behaviours.

The aim in all such individual behaviour plans is to increase the child's behaviour self-awareness and, most of all, *their monitoring and regulating of their own behaviour.* Children are encouraged to look at (and check) their behaviour plan at the beginning of each class period. Their personal copy stays in their locker tray between classes. Some children are comfortable enough to have a postcard-sized and laminated copy of their plan on their table during on-task learning time.

> NB When a copy of the plan is passed on to each specialist colleague (and principal) there are also guidelines on specific ways in which the initiating teacher (normally the grade teacher) has given successful feedback, encouragement and motivation. This is particularly important if visual monitoring (ticks, stamps) and 'rewards' are used.
>
> It is also important that a consistent time-out plan (least-to-most) is communicated to *all* the teachers (and support staff) working with the child (p. 93f).

## Step 6

In the classroom the teacher reminds, encourages and – even – disciplines within the focus of (and language of) the child's 'plan'. If a child is disruptive the teacher will often say, "... What is your plan – *what should you be doing now*?" Again – this raises the child's immediate behaviour awareness and directs the child's focus to *their* plan. 'On the mat' reminders are often given non-verbally (see p. 54).

Encouragement and praise should be brief, specific, regular and *descriptive*. We avoid global praise such as 'great!', 'brilliant' and 'wonderful'. We focus on what the child's effort was relative their behaviour within their plan (see p. 76).[26]

## Rewards

Some teachers include a tick/stamp 'reward' system with the child's plan. Each teacher makes a conscious effort to notice a child's effort and approximation to their plan, and will (one to one) show the child the ticks or stamps corresponding to their effort to remember their plan. Ideally, though, the child needs to get used to verbal encouragement and feedback and the self-reinforcement that peer approval and success generate when a child experiences 'success' in learning and behaviour.

In Jackson's case we saw a significant improvement in his behaviour. There were – naturally – lapses (and bad days). On those days normal, positive, discipline and behaviour consequences were utilised. Each day, though, there was a fresh start; a new day.

## Behaviour agreement for chair rocking

Clarissa (6 years old) was frequently (very frequently) rocking backwards on her chair, hands on table. It was in part attentional behaviour ('notice me everyone' – 'and teacher'!), it was also in part a task-avoidance behaviour. It was also distracting many other children in class. The class teacher had had a couple of chats with her after class time (as well as numerous discipline calls – during seat-work – to 'sit up straight on your chair in class …', to 'get on with your work'). She had tried to be positive with her but was finding the frequent correction wearing; suspecting it was – itself – counter-reinforcing. My colleague and I decided to work on a *personal* behaviour plan with Clarissa.

We set aside some one-to-one time for the class teacher to develop the behaviour plan with Clarissa.

- We used simple picture cues to raise her initial behaviour awareness. The first picture showed Clarissa rocking in her chair during on-task learning time (see Fig. 3).

  We asked her what she thought was happening 'in the picture'. She quickly identified the student in the drawing as herself, "I'm pushing on my chair …". She said this sulkily – no doubt realising it was inappropriate behaviour; discomfort no doubt heightened by the drawing illustrating social disapproval on the teacher's and fellow children's faces.

  Our tone – and manner – throughout were pleasant and consciously focused on helping Clarissa to be behaviourally aware.

Fig. 3

- We – then – briefly *mirrored* Clarissa's frequent kinaesthetic rocking (Fig. 3). She laughed when her teacher 'tried to be her' …
- We showed her a second picture (Fig. 4) illustrating her sitting on her chair ('four-on-the-floor'), and looking 'happy'; her peers (and teacher) also looking 'happy'.

We discussed this second picture as 'her plan' to help her to remember to sit on her seat without rocking (and distracting other children); we explained what we meant by 'distracting' (the mirroring helped, significantly, to symbolise this).

Fig. 4

- Her class teacher then – briefly – modelled 'the plan' (i.e.: how to sit – relaxedly – without rocking ...). We discussed how this 'kind of sitting' would help her with her thinking and her classwork and how it would help her classmates.
- We then practised 'how to sit ...' (as in the picture). She said, "That's easy ...". "Alright ... show me how you can sit, relaxed with *all legs* (chair and yours) on the floor." Clarissa laughed. The 'rehearsal' did not take long. "So Clarissa; *that's your plan* for sitting at your table group in class-work time. Remember – too – if you need my help with any of your work – what do you have to do ...?" She then discussed with Clarissa how to get the teacher's help *fairly* – and why. She also explained that she would put a 'tick' on her copy of Clarissa's plan when she remember to sit (without rocking) and to ask for her teacher's help without calling out.

Back in class Clarissa made a significant effort – she consciously worked on remembering 'her plan'. Her teacher would quietly (and briefly) affirm her effort and (later in the day) gave some one-to-one feedback on her effort using the 'ticks' (on her behaviour plan) to show Clarissa how well she had remembered. When she forgot (and it was – mostly – forgetting) the teacher would non-verbally cue her or go to the table group and ask (quietly) 'What's your plan for sitting and working ...?'

This is an example of how quickly some 'behaviour-recovery' plans can work in improving a child's behaviour awareness and their actual behaviour in class time.

As with all behaviour-recovery plans the class teacher is helping the student (with one-to-one attention) to work on behaviours 'we all do in our class', and supporting the child with in-class encouragement and feedback. The referrant focus for any individual behaviour plan is always the 'classroom behaviour agreement' (outlining the core routines, rules and expected behaviour of all members of 'our class', p. 37f).

> I have found that after the initial introduction and role modelling of the plans, it has been an relatively easy task to encourage teachers to take over the responsibility of using them with their students. I am sure that this is because the teachers have seen the positive outcomes for their students, and they find the plans take away the stress of continually dealing with the perceived negative issues. I have also noticed that the teachers often find that by narrowing down the behaviours and identifying the most urgent ones, they realise that some of the issues are not as significant as they at first thought. (This is always helped by the consistency of colleague support.)
>
> I have found that the quality of the drawings does not matter at all to the child and they hook into the message very quickly. The visual aspect of the plan is non-threatening, simple, factual, and allows the student to begin to take ownership of their behaviours. I always laminate two copies – one for the teacher, and one for the student to place on their desk as a reminder of the steps needed for success. The boxes are ticked by the students, and/or teachers (or teacher-aides), each time the plan is followed. I always talk with the teacher first about making an extra effort at the start to allow for some early success by the child. I have also found that the peer group in the class also 'hook' into the plan and provide positive encouragement to their classmate on the plan.
>
> This method of behaviour recovery has been very successful with the children I have worked with so far. All parties are able to use the plans to work together in a positive way, as a team, to assist success for the child. (Liz – a senior resource teacher for learning and behaviour.)

## "Do you know what your David did ...?!"

One of the more annoying comments heard in some primary schools is, "You know what *your* David did in the playground?!" The implication being that it is, somehow, *the class teacher's* fault that David ('her David') behaved badly in the playground. When *any* teacher is on playground duty it is their responsibility to immediately address inappropriate and wrong behaviour. All teachers, at all times, (even when not on *rostered* duty) need to exercise relaxed vigilance in their duty-of-care role in non-classroom settings. It is unfair, unreasonable and unnecessary to impute blame to a class teacher for the behaviour of any one of her children *outside* a classroom setting.

We have (fortunately) worked in schools where the collegial ethos in out-of-class settings is "When a child is difficult, disturbing, disruptive and even dangerous he is *'everybody's child'* ..."; and they mean it. Of course, any follow-up of critical behaviour issues (post-classroom) should engage the understanding and support of class teachers, but any behaviour planning, or programme, for challenging student behaviour particularly in *non-class settings* is a collegial – whole-school – matter.

## "He's alright with me!"

Some senior teachers will trot this one out when a particularly challenging student has had a one-to-one 'session' with – say – a headteacher. Why wouldn't the very challenging student be 'OK' in the headteacher's office – with an audience of one?

Back in the classroom with his audience of peers it is often a different matter. Attentionally challenging children will 'feed off' their class peers' responses and reactions. As Rudolf Dreikurs et al. (1982) noted in his research, some children's frequency of disruptive behaviour is an expression of their need (in effect) their 'goal' to belong to the social group. A child's overly attentional behaviour is often reinforced by the peer (and adult) acknowledgement in class; whether 'negative' teacher correction, or overly cajoling, or over-attentive teacher dialogue, or peer laughter.

Even if it is true that the colleague in question does 'not have a problem' (with a particular child, or even a *particular class*) it hardly helps! The teacher, struggling with challenging child behaviour, is likely to quickly self-judge – rating themselves against the more successful teacher ('I'm inadequate', 'I can't manage ...', 'I'm not a good teacher', 'It's my fault'). Worse, they are less likely to ask for (or accept) any useful support options proffered by those colleagues who could help.

Colleague support is always more productive when offered in a climate of non-judgemental co-operation; a co-operation based on a knowledge of the demands, hour-by-hour (day-by-day), *of 20 plus children* (in the same room). It only takes one child with challenging (or disordered) behaviour to significantly exacerbate normative stress for the teacher (and the bulk of the children). It is ill-considered, perhaps thoughtless, for a senior teacher to imply that *they* 'do not' (or would not) 'have a problem with this child ...'.

## Temper and frustration tolerance

Kelly (aged 4 years and 6 months) – at pre-school – struggled to cope with her feelings of frustration, anger and (at times) her rage. At primary school it was no better.

Several times a week she would get *so* frustrated she would lash out, or push others and shout at them. Sometimes she would spit, or even bite, when very angry.

Her teacher would organise time-out for her both in class and out of class (p. 99f). She had spoken at length with the mother and was aware of serious predisposing concerns at home but realised that if she was actually going to help Kelly she would have to teach her how to cope with her feelings *at school*. While poor frustration tolerance can be a generalised (even habitual) feature of a child's behaviour, it may also be triggered by factors in the home environment that we (as teachers) clearly have no direct control over. Kelly's teacher was well aware of this.

Kelly's individual behaviour plan followed the practices outlined earlier in this chapter including some gentle 'mirroring' (p. 90). We are always sensitive about mirroring a child's aberrant behaviour. If we believe (or even intuitively feel) that mirroring will only compound a child's anxiety *or* resistance, we focus on utilising illustrations that portray a child's behaviour and our ability to *describe* behaviours. These illustrations act as a 'social-story' (p. 115).

Most children are 'comfortable' with a teacher's mirroring of their behaviour; always conducted in good faith and *always* with a request for permission to show them what 'it looks like when you ...' (p. 116f). We discussed with the team-leader the possibility of including some mirroring and thought it would help if two teachers could *briefly* act out Kelly's typical behaviour as to 'another child'. It was quite effective. It immediately recalled an incident the previous day of snatching a felt-tipped pen (instead of Kelly asking). Kelly had (on that occasion) ended up hitting and spitting at the other child and (consequently) had ended up in time-out – yet again and in tears.

In Kelly's case the behaviour-recovery focused on *teaching* several 'social survival behaviours'. In a child's terms this means learning to:

- *Recognise the 'feeling inside'* (the frustration feeling), and knowing that this is a 'feeling I have' – it does not mean 'I *have* to 'snatch', 'grab', 'hit', 'push', 'spit' or 'bite' *when* I have that feeling ...'.
- What to do, and what sorts of things to say *when* 'that feeling' comes. We modelled and practised saying things that related to:
  – asking before (and if) you want to borrow *and* giving back after having borrowed (instead of snatching or grabbing);
  – saying 'please' and 'thanks'/'ta';
  – saying 'excuse me' when moving through/past someone else in class;
  – if someone is doing something/or saying something you don't like (or 'upsets

you') say, "I don't like it when you …" Here the teacher practised some common examples emphasising what sorts of things to say, and 'how' to say them (and not shouting!). *And*, if the other children don't listen, come and see your teacher (or the teaching assistant).

These behaviours, and positive language cues, seem so basic; for some children, however, they need an *individual* and positive teaching focus that behaviour recovery can provide. Kelly was able to identify with these behaviours, and back in class was both encouraged, and quietly disciplined (when necessary), within her plan. One of the common – quiet – discipline asides we use in such cases is to simply ask the child, "What is your plan? What should you be doing now?" If the child is too distressed, of course, we engage distractions or diversions or time-out.

Of course it takes commitment and perseverance by a teacher for such 'plans' to succeed. An essential key to any success with such plans is the quality of the relationship of teacher(s) (and teacher assistants) who support and encourage the child. In Kelly's case, it was 'three steps forward one step back', but over a four-week period there was a significant improvement in her classroom behaviour. It was patently obvious – purely from the lack of need for time-out – that she was improving within a fortnight. What was a joy to see was Kelly as a much happier child at school, and particularly the positive response by her classmates to her efforts to change her behaviour.

NB We always emphasise to the child in our one-to-one feedback sessions that *they* are changing *their* behaviour. We are helping them, of course, but it is *they* who are 'remembering' to …(i.e., their 'plan').

Our goal in supporting the child is always to enable them to:

- Understand, and be aware of, their behaviour and its effect on themselves and others (including their teacher). We do this not to entertain guilt but to raise reciprocal awareness of others and (in time) perspective-taking and empathy to others.
- Own and monitor and – in a sense – 'regulate' their own behaviour instead of having an adult (seemingly) constantly telling them 'how to behave'.[27]

# Anger

## Angry and aggressive children

When were you last really angry? – not just annoyed, irritated, or a little frustrated but *angry*(!!). Anger is the most extreme of our emotions; while it can drive us to meet what we believe is our 'fight for justice', it can also drive us to do and say hurtful, destructive, things; even to those we love. Understanding our own anger (as adults) and the difficulty of its management is an important prerequisite for helping children understand their frustration, anger and aggression. If we find it hard – at times – how hard must it be for them?

## When a child behaves with aggressive anger

While a teacher should always be empathetic about the difficult, and dysfunctional, circumstances that predispose some children's behaviour, we should never tolerate, or play down, or excuse lashing out by kicking, screaming, yelling, abusive swearing, spitting, throwing objects.

When a child 'stabs' another on the arm with a pencil, or threatens another child with scissors, or purposefully pushes, or trips, or punches – because they don't like, or are frustrated by, another child – we should quickly, firmly, assertively address such behaviour. We do this to communicate to the individual that such *behaviour* is unacceptable and will not be tolerated; we also do this because of the 'audience of peers' needs to hear, and see, adult protective leadership.

It is essential that children are not told they are 'bad' for getting angry or that 'it's wrong for them to get/be angry'. All of us get angry at times. Anger is an emotion (or at least, at times, a transitory feeling). We cannot actually *stop* frustration coming to us.

In some people, however, the 'psychological space' between the feeling of frustration and the expression of frustration or anger is very small!

What is helpful in life is to learn what to do or say *when* we have those high level feelings of frustration, or anger. This is in part aided (or hampered) by temperament but it is also aided by *learning skills of frustration tolerance*. Children can learn these skills with appropriate, positive, adult support and teaching.

The skills relevant at early years level involve *recognition and awareness* of frustration (a crucial 'skill' even in adults!); being aware of tension in one's body and 'stirred-up feelings inside' and learning (correspondingly) to relax tense muscles and breathe slower (and paced). It is also important to learn what sorts of things to say to someone if, and when, you are upset, annoyed or angry with them.

More difficult to teach (but none the less important) is teaching children a *basic* vocabulary of emotion. When children get annoyed, or frustrated (even in a learning task), they will often (and naturally) use global black/white emotional language, "I'm angry because I can't do the work ...", "I *hate* this work ...", "I'll *never* be able to do it ...". Learning to understand the basic *degree* of emotion can help children see the appropriate difference between concern, annoyance, frustration, upset(edness) and more intense emotions such as anger. Anger is a much 'bigger' emotion (in terms of 'emotional weight'). Children can learn to describe their degree of frustration more helpfully (for them and their teacher).

## Time-out

Cool-off time is often essential for *very* frustrated or angry children. It is pointless trying to get to 'the reasons' for their hostile or aggressive – angry – behaviour in the heat of the moment. Cool-off time should be exercised calmly, respectfully, firmly, decisively (in-class cool-off time or exit from the class if necessary).It is crucial to have a whole-school plan for *any* use of 'time-out' (p. 93f).

## Longer-term support

Any longer-term support should have – as its aim – teaching children to understand and be aware of their feelings and emotions; to learn to communicate how *intensely* they feel (without resorting to verbal or physical aggression wherever possible ...); to learn a 'vocabulary of emotion' (Rogers, 2003a) to label their feelings and express how much they feel. They also need to learn strategies, and skills, to manage their anger or cope with others' anger.

At some stage (after cool-off time) it will be important to follow-up with a child to increase their understanding about anger-*feeling* and anger-*behaviour*. It is important to *briefly* tune into a child's feelings *when* they are angry and help the child to refocus appropriate behaviour, or (if they are *too* emotionally 'worked-up') organise 'cool-off time'.

Later the teacher can spend more focused time, one-to-one, with the child: "I can see you're very annoyed (upset, concerned, frustrated, fed-up, angry) ..." By tuning into a child's probable feelings we help them with short-term self-awareness and some self-control.

Essentially it is *acknowledging* their feelings; not saying we 'understand' how they feel or, necessarily, approve.

When a teacher says to a child, "To have someone say things like that can be ..." (here we name the feeling e.g.: frustrating, annoying, upsetting, hurtful ...), this can help make it easier for the child to believe their teacher understands and can help them learn more appropriate ways of expressing anger than just lashing out, or physically hurting others (tempting as it is at times!). Denying a child's feelings is tantamount to judging a child. Before we can help them (long term) with more appropriate 'emotional behaviour' we need to demonstrate we can, and will, listen (at a calmer moment).

- Teach the child about the links between angry *thinking*, angry *feelings* and angry *behaviour* (simple drawings, even safe role-play can all help here).
- Explain and model that angry thinking ("I *hate* him!!" *All* teachers are ...!!") affects *how* frustrated or angry we feel (this is particularly helpful for older children).
- Teach the child strategies for 'self-calming' (relaxation words, clench/unclench face (and fists!), counting backwards from ten, calm breathing).
- Some children (at this age) are also able to learn to sub-vocalise self-calming statements (Rogers, 2003a). The teacher practises this with the child aloud and then teaches how to 'sub-vocalise' ("helpful talk to talk inside your head ...").

Children get frustrated or 'angry' for similar reasons to those of adults : normal life frustrations, difficulty with required tasks, conflict over possessions; verbal abuse (put-downs, lying about someone, tale-telling), physical hurt or abuse ... (Marion, 2000; Rogers, 2003a).

A key feature of *'aggressive anger'* is the build-up of frustration and the feeling of 'losing control'; some children (and adults) have a very low tolerance to frustration. It can help if a teacher notices a child easily, quickly, getting angry to quietly tune into the child's probable emotional state and acknowledge (and name) what they are probably feeling. A child may also need to be refocused, or re-directed, to appropriate behaviour, or may even need cool-off time until they can gain self-control.

There is a very helpful picture-story book for children, *Danny in the Toy Box* (Tulloch and Greder, 1990), about a little boy who gets very *cross* and how he handles his temper. Its gentle and realistic humour can help children (and adults) gain an insight into this strong emotion.

It is also important to distinguish between the occasional angry outburst and the *characteristic* expressions of inappropriate anger behaviour. Some children will benefit from an individual behaviour management plan where they are taught:

- That anger as a 'feeling' is not bad; we *all* get angry.
- The *do* bit of anger (how we think, what we think, how we behave with words and actions) is something we can change for the better; "better for us, better for others."
- Help the child to be aware of situations and circumstances that lower their tolerance to frustration; an anger-diary can help to chart the 'trigger factors' ... (Rogers, 2003a). Self-awareness is a key step in self-monitoring and self-directing behaviour.

- Give the child key 'words' or 'phrases' he can say to himself *and* others when he is upset, annoyed, irritated, frustrated or even angry. "I feel …"; "I don't like it when …"; "I am angry because …"; "I don't want you to …".
- Rehearse and practise (one to one) (p. 118).
- Boys will sometimes think it is weak not to hit out at others when they feel aggressive. It is important to assure them it is OK (not 'weak') to ask an adult (a teacher or aide) to help out when they feel frustrated or angry … "Sean, we all get angry feelings sometimes …". We find it helpful to indicate some non-verbal cues here to simulate the emotion of anger by a 'frown', by a 'churning motion near the tummy' …, 'clenched fists and jaw' … "Have you noticed what you do – and say – when you feel like that …?" This can help the child be aware what he then *normally* does when he feels like that and the effect it has on others.
- Encourage their efforts at positive anger-management.
- On occasions mediation strategies can help when a child's frustration leads to angry verbal or physical behaviour towards another child (or teacher). After ample cool-off time the mediation process can enable the child concerned to understand the effect his behaviour has on others' feelings, and to know that while such angry *behaviour* is wrong he (as a person) is not rejected; that a relationship can be re-established and that (where appropriate) restitution may be required.

While it is obvious that some children will have less positive experiences and 'adult role models' regarding expressing feelings of frustration and anger, teachers can greatly assist children's awareness about their feelings through whole-class dialogue; positive stories, classroom-meetings, learning relaxation skills, positive discipline and *individual* behaviour plans.

It was so encouraging when one of my 5-year-old children went from an initial (and frequent) "I'm going to burn this f—ing school down", to finding his school an enjoyable and *safe* haven.

These skills (particularly relaxation skills) can also be taught in whole-class games and activities. See the excellent text by Jenny Rickard, *Relaxation for Children* (1994).

## Children's expressions of their feelings

Learning to trust a new – significant – adult is an essential part of a child's development at school. Communicating feelings, particularly feelings of anxiety and significant frustration, are difficult for young children.

It is important that children know, and feel, they are allowed to *be* anxious, even angry, and they are not 'bad' or 'weak' because of this. Some children are acutely anxious because of a fear of failure in learning tasks. The teacher's ability to tune into (privately and quietly) to a child's feelings, and to provide assurance, will go a long way to allaying such anxiety. Children can also benefit by having an appropriate class buddy who can encourage and assist with learning tasks.

Children can only do this when they are treated by adults in a supportive way, that allows validation of unpleasant, uncomfortable and even frightening emotions. This opportunity to access and communicate feelings and emotions can range from the death of a pet, to a family crisis; from uncertainty about learning to teasing, friendship concerns and bullying.

Teachers are also confidantes to a range of emotional concerns (from home and at school) and we need, at all times, to be aware of the ethical obligation that occasions our role in that regard.

We should never try to force a child to talk about their feelings even when they are visibly upset – (perhaps *especially* when they are visibly upset). At that time they will need our calm reassurance; a tissue; some cool-off-time and the assurance that we can talk about this when they have calmed down.

We enable children's trust by:

- Sensing when a child is having a bad-day or looks troubled.
- Tuning incidentally or directly into, a child's feelings. "Perhaps you're feeling …"; "You look upset (or concerned, or annoyed … [whatever]".
- Offering a child some considered options: 'cool-off-time'; talking through a problem, or with a child who has been hurt by another (verbally or physically).
- Reframing the situation for the child when they see only the worst, or the most terrible, before them.
- Focus on the child's present/future (we do not hold grudges with children, nor do we hark back to yesterday's or last week's bad behaviour).

If children are not allowed (or do not have the opportunity) to express their anxious, or angry, feelings about an issue or relationship it will clearly affect their ongoing learning, behaviour and social relationships.

## Specialist help

There are children whose socio-emotional behaviour seems unresponsive to the sorts of support we (as teachers, as a school community) would normally offer. There are children whose causative pathology (p. 109f) is so traumatic that – at best – the school's support options only hold aberrant (and dysfunctional) behaviour in check.

Some children will need specialist counselling; either psychological, medical, or psychiatric support. Any child we suspect of being seriously at risk will need that wider support network. We also need to engage parents/carers (and appropriate authorities) when we are concerned that a child is significantly at risk. Obviously any decision to broach such concerns with a parent/carer, or the authorities (say in suspected abuse) needs to be made with senior teacher support.

It is essential we keep careful records of the features (and contexts) of aberrant, and dysfunctional, behaviour to assist welfare, counselling and medical agencies. Such records will also be crucial in parent/carer and education authority meetings to discuss behaviour and learning concerns.

# Chapter 7

## Working with parents/carers using the classroom behaviour agreement

### Parents/carers

Imagine yourself as a parent/carer going to a new school with your 4- or 5-year-old? How do *you* feel as an adult at that first meeting?

How we establish – and seek to maintain – positive and supportive links with parents and carers will have a crucial role in the child's learning and behaviour at school. Like many parents and carers, we have both been through this experience, and even as *an adult* it is not easy to divorce first impressions from how they affect beliefs about *this particular place* called school. Of course those first impressions can be wrong but – in children – it is hard for them to deny how they feel as a kind of proof of 'what is' at school. If you are a parent or carer and you have been through this:

■ How were you treated – spoken to – by the first adult you met at the school: by the class teacher? … by the senior staff? How did that first contact affect how you felt about *this place*? Did those feelings change over time – how?
■ In some primary schools older children (as with teachers) are involved in the greeting/welcoming of parents/carers and the 'school tour'.
■ What did the teacher/s *actually do* to enable you to feel 'at ease'; accepted; allowed to ask even 'dumb' questions without feeling stupid or inadequate (like you may have felt all those years ago when you first walked through the school gate at 4 or 5 years of age)?

We say we want (the) school to be a place where children can feel safe; feel accepted, valued and included. We hope – too – the parents/carers will sense, appreciate and feel something of this in their first meetings with the school administration and (most of all) by their child's class teacher.

Parents/carers sometimes feel patronised, 'looked-down-upon' by teachers (*some* teachers); as if they could not know anything about the real – and complex – workings of a school. We too (as teachers and as parents) have both felt that with *some* teachers in *some* school settings. While this is human nature, it does alert us – as teachers – to how parents/carers may have heightened feelings (from their own memories of school) as they make their first excursions to school as a parent or carer.

Then, of course, there are those parents/carers who know all about the 'do's' and 'don't's' of teaching. They know 'what it's all about' – they could do your job in their sleep (after all they did go to school for 13 years!).

They are – primarily – thinking about the welfare of their children. Will they be safe here? Will the teachers be kind, perceptive, firm (when necessary)? How will they communicate fair rules? What kind of rules does the school (and *this* class teacher) have here? How do they discipline? … encourage? … affirm our children?

Parents/carers are also – in a sense – 'going to school' as well.

As well as wanting a 'good teacher' for their child, the parents/carers of early years children often expect the class teacher to be a kind of 'second mum'.

Many children – certainly – will soon relate to their grade teacher as a 'second mother'. Anxieties, frustrations, cuts and bruises – we are *in loco parentis*, most acutely, with children when they come to a school as new entrants.

There is also the parental/carer sub-culture outside the classroom. Parents/carers comparing their child's reading ages and abilities(!) – what they should be able to do 'by now?', and "Do you know what so-and-so dressed their child like?!"

There can be – among some – a residual competitiveness. I actually had a mother from my class go up to a mother from another class and tell her that her daughter was 'stupid' because she should be well past level 1 readers by now. I never really imagined that I would ever have to call a mother into my office to be reprimanded (I mean have a focused, respectful, clarifying chat!) (Elizabeth).

We cannot *guarantee* a child's happiness while they are with us; we cannot guarantee they will learn (in the formal 3Rs sense); we cannot even guarantee they will always feel safe, or *be* safe, while with us. We can – and must – enable an environment likely *to create conditions for* likely happiness, learning, inclusion and safety.

The classroom behaviour agreement will go a long way to informing and explaining what we mean (as a school community) by those enabling conditions (p. 37f). The classroom behaviour agreement gives both an initial, and a subsequent, bridge of shared understanding between home and school.

Whenever we discipline a child publicly or one to one; whenever we follow-through with a consequence or punishment, it can help to *imagine* the parent/carer 'sitting-in' – how would I then speak to the child …? relate to the child?

This is not an artificial 'exercise'; it is a reminder that we have an acute responsibility in discipline contexts (particularly when we need to be assertively firm). A responsibility to balance dignified treatment and necessary discipline.

Imagine too (if you can): How would we (as a child) generally feel about being in a classroom where we were the teacher. Bad-day notwithstanding of course (p. 6)!

## Parent/carer support

In the establishment phase of the year we will be meeting many caring and 'keen' parents/carers as they bring their children to the classroom door. Some seem overly protective. If we are parents/carers we remember our child's first days at school – our natural protectiveness, anxieties and concerns. What will our daughter's teacher be like? Kind? Fair? Strict? – How strict? In what way? Will my daughter, my son, make friends? How will she/he fit in …? How 'good' a teacher is Ms Smith?

## The 45-minute goodbye

Some parents/carers, however, are overly anxious, as well as overly protective. The child clings to their mother (it is most often the mother) crying – and the tears are real (not manufactured). Some parents (naturally) want to reassure their child; some will overly reassure. "YES!! I love you my sweetie. No, no mummy won't leave; no. Don't cry – please don't cry! It's going to be lovely here – isn't it?" They turn anxiously to the teacher, "Mummy will be back; I PROMISE …" – and so it goes on.

It is important to – calmly, kindly, reassuringly – break into this extended goodbye. "Mrs Smith, It will be alright. I'll take Daniel now." Then – a *quiet aside to the mother* – "He'll be alright soon. It's natural that he's anxious. In half an hour please feel free to call the school and check. It will be better – now – if you just say goodbye to Daniel, and then leave and walk off in a confident way (without looking back). I know it's not easy. Please trust us. Thank you."

It can be heart-wrenching for a parent or carer on the first day (or, sometimes, the first week or so) to see their child actually sobbing – 'heaving' – and not want to protect them by 'staying'. In my first year of teaching I had a boy who used to cry and claw at the classroom door because he did not want to leave his little brother from another class. I also had a little boy (4 years and 6 months) who hid under the computer table almost every lesson, of every day, in the first few weeks of term. With parental discussion, one-to-one reassurance and amazing peer tolerance from the rest of the class, he settled in and became a confident and positive child – thoroughly enjoying his time at school.

The teacher's reassuring manner is crucial here – on the child (and the parent's/carer's) first day; it will have a lasting impression. As the mother leaves we escort Daniel (by the hand) to a couple of socially confident – and kind – children as we start to harness the group together in that first calming group-time (see p. 107f).

## Inside the classroom?

Some schools have a clear policy that mothers (or fathers or other care-givers) leave their children at the classroom door; it can get very crowded in a classroom when half a dozen parents/carers co-alesce; distracting, chatting, 'fussing' …

If parents/carers are crowding the doorway, a little – respectful – 'reminding' will help. "Excuse me everyone – it's getting a little crowded at the door here …"

Our polite courtesy (the confident, expectant tone and smile) is crucial here – we need to convey purpose and 'necessity', not 'bossiness'.

We will obviously encourage parental supporters to work in the classroom (later in the term – when the class group is established). Any policy of parent/carer support and involvement in working with children must be based on *a whole-school policy* and not merely left to the discretion of the class teacher.[28]

## The classroom behaviour agreement

By the end of the first week teachers ought to have their published *classroom behaviour agreement* in place (p. 37f). The photographs of the children – illustrating the rules and responsibilities – in this agreement will go a long way to clarifying our expectations to parents and carers about behaviour within the school community. (See appendix B)

The classroom agreement is also a basis for *any* dialogue, or concern, a parent or carer (or teacher) has about a child's behaviour at school (Chapter 3).

On our first parent/carer–teacher 'information night' the 'classroom agreement' concept – its meaning and usage – will form a crucial part of our presentation and discussion about behaviour and learning.

Concepts like 'discipline', 'consequences' and 'punishment' – as well as the more pedestrian expectations about rules and routines – need to be clarified and *relevant* examples given.

## Essential areas that will always improve communication, assurance and support between parents/carers and the school

- We need to pay particular attention to (and emphasis on) the entrance of our school and the welcoming classroom door. These 'first-places' convey a lot aesthetically, as well as in a sense of 'this-is-a-place-I'd-like-my-child-to-be …'.
- We will take care to have organised space and place emphasis in the classroom. A messy, disorganised, aesthetically boring classroom will give an immediate negative impression to most parents/carers. That first welcoming, positive 'look' and 'feel' of a classroom is crucial. Obviously this has to be more than mere show (and if it is not, parents/carers – and children – will soon know it!)
- Many schools have a welcome pack for the parents/carers of early years age children (or children new to the school). A *user-friendly* handbook (with photographs), a useful *and clear map*; the *timing* of the school day (basic, but essential); the names of the child's subject (as well as class) teachers; particular protocols about sun awareness, toilet procedures and the like …

  Particular policy imperatives that address behaviour and bullying are noted in this 'handbook'. Parents/carers will also (in the first week or two) receive a copy of the classroom behaviour agreement (Chapter 3).

  Schools often have a short CD presentation for new parents/carers that gives an overall impression of 'our school'. It is often shown at the first parent/carer information meeting (or can be loaned out).
- A regular classroom newsletter from the *class* teacher is a common feature in primary schools generally. This should also include information from subject teachers from time to time. Parents/carers will often read a *class* newsletter from 'their' teacher in preference to most school notices (no offence!).
- Protocols for contacting a teacher. While this is included in the booklet it will sometimes need to be tactfully spelled out to some parents/carers who think they ought to have immediate access to their child's teacher (at any time).
- It is crucial to clarify pick-up times at the end of the school day – and who picks up whom. Protocols of signing in (particularly if it is not the immediate parent/carer) need to be clarified on day one; even if we have already spelled this out at our first meeting with new entrant parents and carers.
- Many schools now have a care-givers room where parents and carers can relax, meet, chat, have a cup of tea/coffee.
- Parents/carers should be made aware of the school's peer-buddy programme on day one (p. 35f).
- Some teachers have a post-it box (for parental/carer concerns), or a clipboard (outside their classroom door) for parents/carers to note an issue, question or concern that might occasion more than a 'quick word at the door'.

■ The men's breakfast meeting: Many schools have found it helpful to conduct a special 'men's get-together – breakfast' (early enough in term one – a poll will help here). At the 'breakfast meet' the issues 'more particular' to male parent/care-givers can be raised and discussed.

It is important that this form of meeting is not merely a 'blokey' get-together. What such a meeting can provide is context of 'gender commonality'. It is not always easy to get male care-givers to such meetings. This kind of forum – thoughtfully advertised (with issues relevant to male parents/carers) – can be a useful adjunct to normative parent/carer meetings.

## Communication

One of the best lessons I learnt way back on my teaching internship, was the importance of communication and being prepared (Elizabeth). Children take comfort in being prepared, having rules and guidelines and knowing what to expect. A big part of being prepared for the regular (and irregular) routines of the week, is communication with parents/carers. I used to keep a folder of laminated signs to keep on the classroom door (where parents/carers would see it) for all occasions:

■ 'Art tomorrow, remember to bring your art smocks'.
■ 'Library day tomorrow, remember to bring your library bags and books.'
■ 'Swimming starts tomorrow, remember to bring your towel, bathers etc.'
■ 'Sport tomorrow, please remember to put appropriate footwear on your child.'
■ 'It's going to be 42 degrees today; please feel free to pick your child up early.'
■ 'Our excursion is coming up soon, have you returned your permission slip and payment?'

I also had a whiteboard in the alcove outside our classroom where I would post interesting articles relevant to reception class (4 to rising 5s) children, sign-up sheets for parent/carer, birthday messages, etc.

Simple things like making sure the newsletter and notices actually end up at home may seem obvious but these deceptively simple strategies can make sure they are more likely to get there.

Some teachers find it helpful to provide a communication folder, or a pocket inside the child's 'take home book' folder.

It also helps to clip spare newsletters/notices to the classroom door, or the communication board, or a spot in the classroom where parents/carers know they can go, like a spare tub.

Children feel more confident when they are prepared and know what to expect.

For early years children, their parents/carers have to be a big part of that process, so keeping them informed is important.

Each afternoon, I would go through *tomorrow's plan* with the children as we were winding down the day, bags packed and sitting on the floor ready to go home. I would go over 'what tomorrow had in store', even if it was something as simple as re-capping the letter of the week or something we were learning about that they could share with their families.

## Safety

I am very concerned and focused on the safety of my children. I would count my children in the classroom, as they were getting on the bus, as they got off the bus, while we were at the excursion (especially swimming), as we got back on the bus, when we got off the bus and when we got back to our classroom. Obsessive? Maybe, but as a teacher we are in charge of someone's 'world'; someone's very reason for living – their child.

One afternoon when the children had been dismissed, a grandmother came into the classroom looking for her grandson and we could not find him. We asked the children who were still in the playground, we searched everywhere, we called the parents (straight to voice-mail) we then drove around the local shops to check if the grandfather had picked him up by mistake. We ended up calling the police – as a precaution – and I drove, with the grandmother, to the child's house. The mother answered the door and I glanced past her to see her son sitting on the couch watching television. She had picked him up as usual, the grandmother had just got her days wrong and it was not her turn to pick him up that day. Well I just walked to the end of the veranda and burst into tears. That still ranks as one of the worst teaching days of my life (Elizabeth).

From then on I was really vigilant with making sure each child was paired to their parent/carer as they left my care at the classroom door. I kept an area of the 'carpet board' that had the heading 'Where are you going after school?' I had icons for after-school care, tennis and one for 'if someone different was picking them up', then I would put their names beside the appropriate icon. I would also make sure the after-school club children walked over to the building in a group where I could watch them go. Then, when everyone had gone home, I would go over to the after-school club, check on my children and pass on any relevant information to the staff. I also had icons on the board under the title 'Where are you?' If the children were off to the toilet, gifted programme, children's council,[29] running errands, they would take their name off the board and velcro it to the icon and we could see at a glance who was out of the room and where they were.

# Parental/carer awareness of discipline

We come across many parents/carers who still see discipline – primarily – in *punitive* terms (so too with consequences). It is important to clarify (without sounding 'preachy') what we mean, and emphasise, when we discipline children. We try to communicate that discipline is essentially *how we* lead, guide, encourage their children to control *their* own behaviour in a way that respects others.

One of the ways we have found helpful to illustrate this understanding is to demonstrate – at a targeted parent/carer/teacher evening – three alternate 'styles' of discipline: the authoritarian/'bossy', the non-assertive and the authoritative/assertive. Teachers take on mini role-plays to illustrate how different language expression (and voice, tone, and body language) can affect *what* a child hears, and how children normally respond to the differing approaches. We then invite parental/carer responses as to why children might respond differently to the discipline 'styles' we present. The visual modelling is extremely powerful; particularly for the potential 'know-all (even belligerent) parent/carer' who thinks we should bring back guard dogs, gun turrets, barbed wire as well as corporal punishment into schools. The most often repeated phrase here is, "It didn't do me any harm!" A discussion on the difference between *certainty* and *severity* of behaviour consequences is always well received at this point (p. 51). We also model the difference between mere punishment and behaviour consequences (typical examples are given) replete with knowing laughter.

# Hostile, angry or aggressive parents/carers[30]

If any parent/carer appears at our classroom door with evident hostile, or aggressive, body language, or threatening language, it is crucial that we immediately send for senior teacher support (whether in class time or non-contact time).

There are parents/carers who will sidestep any protocols about 'seeing a teacher' (whenever *they* feel like it!). They will by-pass the front office and make a bee-line for the classroom (even if the teacher is teaching).

It is crucial, firstly, to send a trusted child across to the teacher nearby (to communicate to that teacher) that adult assistance is required immediately. In some schools there is a small laminated red card in every room (with the room number on). The red card signals to senior staff that adult assistance is required immediately. Fortunately with mobile phones (and class phones) these days this call for assistance is much easier. We should not underestimate how disturbing – even distressing – this can be in some schools.

Ideally parents/carers should make an appointment with their class teacher (via the administration). With the more hostile parent/carer it is crucial that a senior teacher sits in on any such meetings. The senior teacher's presence is as part 'advo-cate for the teacher', part moral support, and to present the *appropriately formal and official* face of the school to the parent/carer.

The difficulty with the more hostile parent/carer ("He was alright at the last 15 schools! It's just since he came to this s--t school!") is to keep the fundamental respect intact and present a calm, 'professional' focus.

We may well feel like saying, "Was he just Mrs Whinger! He was fine at the last 15 schools? Was he just!! Well he is a little ... here! And no wonder with a mother like you! You go home; you take a valium sandwich and you come back *when* you can do so without yelling, swearing and threatening me!!" But we cannot do that. It is that passing – brief – tempting thought though. We have had colleagues say, "Can't I say that once? *Just once!*" It is *never* worth it, nor is it appropriate or necessary; just a trifle tempting.

What is crucial in any such meeting (unplanned or planned) is our ability to communicate calmness and take control of the 'meeting' (we cannot, obviously, control the irate parent/carer).

- We may need to let the parent/carer 'run-out-of-steam' for a minute or two (without looking at our watch).
- Then direct them to a seat and *briefly* tune into how we think we believe they may be feeling at this point (about their child's detention, 'punishment', rumoured bullying – whatever ...).
- Assure them that we know they care, "I know you care about Tyson; you wouldn't be here if you didn't. We care too ..." ('not much' – you might feel like saying on occasion).
- "Mrs Smith (calmly), I'm not yelling at you or swearing. I don't expect you to swear at me. As I said, I can see you're upset. Let's talk about what happened ..." At this point it is important to *focus on the current* (present) issue, behav-iour or concern about the child and not get dragged into the 'past' (even the child's past at *this* school let alone at the last 15 schools!)
- If the parent/carer prevaricates, exaggerates, misconstrues or misrepresents the truth it is important to keep the focus on the child's behaviour and his needs.
- We will reference the *classroom behaviour agreement* as it affects (and is affected by) the child's behaviour. The central focus being how the child's *behaviour* affects learning, or safety, or the fair treatment of others or others' property, or school property ...
- We should never apologise for, or mitigate, the essential and non-negotiable rights inherent in our policy as they affect safety and learning. We will need (for example) to clarify the *non-negotiable nature* of bullying and due consequences (immediate time-out, even temporary exclusion from school) with subsequent

due process of mediation and monitoring of the student's behaviour.

This is crucial when addressing the parents/carers of hostile, aggressive, violent children and bullying children.

- While giving parents/carers appropriate (and necessary) right-of-reply, we should also not let them dominate a meeting, or continue to threaten – *ever*.
- If the parent/carer refuses to work though a reason(able) due process we will need to close the meeting – decisively – and 'reschedule' (directing them to leave and, when they are calmer – more settled, make an appointment to talk things through …).

The aim of any meeting should, at least, be to allow a parent/carer to air their concern (fairly and reasonably) and look for a fair and workable solution.

Often such a meeting will recommend a behaviour-recovery approach (a personal behaviour agreement, mediation process or restitution.)

## Parent/carer/teacher interviews (Elizabeth)

I have heard some pretty 'full on' ideas about what people do for parent/carer/-teacher interviews ranging from face-to-face across the table with parents and carers in a hall full of teachers and parents/carers lined up in a production line … to teachers preparing classical music, vases of flowers, oil burners, sitting around a table with the child in question. We need to take into account 'the done thing' in our own school. What worked for me was having my classroom looking aesthetically pleasing and positive, having examples of the children's work marked with Post-it notes and being as prepared as I could be.

I had notes on my lap-top with reminders about each family, … parents'/carers' names, occupations, names of siblings, where they lived, major issues relating to the child, points to focus on, etc.

I put my notes on the lap-top in the order of the interviews, had a copy of their child's report with me, any individual behaviour plans, copies of additional reports (etc.) with water and disposable cups and tissues on hand.

Parents/carers sometimes get emotional when it comes to their children. If we are expecting an aggressive, hostile or overly talkative parent/carer, we will need to give our principal a copy of our interview timetable and highlight the timeslot and name where we are expecting possible trouble. Our principal can then stick their head into our classroom and we can give them a nod if we are having trouble. Our principal can then say something along the lines of, "I'm sorry, we're going to have to wrap this up, I need to borrow Miss Smith for something …". You get the idea.

# Notes

1. Early years teachers, particularly at pre-school and reception, often use the affectional (and protective) possessive pronoun when referring to individuals and their classes; it is "*my* Sean" or "*our* Sean ...", "*our* Melissa ...", "*my* class ...", "*our* class".

2. The use of the term 'discipline' is not necessarily the educational 'flavour of the month'. There is often a negative association with this term; understandably. My own experiences (noted briefly in this book) regarding discipline are mostly negative – often harsh, punitive, even cruel. We have sought to carefully, and (we hope) productively, reinvest this word with its appropriate meaning to guide, lead and enable a child's self-control *as well as* the need for appropriate behaviour consequences.

   Behaviour management is a broader term that embraces organisational and time management *as well as 'discipline'*, or it may delineate the necessary corrective aspect of our behaviour leadership.

3. This book takes a duly conscious account of children's emotional, physical, psychological and moral development – at early years. The focus of the book, however, is not on child development *per se* but on the dignified, appropriate and necessary behaviour management and discipline practice in early years.

   There are many excellent texts that address a child's psychological and social development. Of particular note is the book by Jennie Lindon, *Understanding Child Development: Linking Theory and Practice* (2007).

4. I borrowed this phrase from Patrick White's very moving novel, *Riders in the Chariot* (Penguin Modern Classics), 1961, p. 224.

5. 'Corporal' meaning punishment inflicted on the human body. Corporal punishment was abolished in the mid-1980s in most western countries (1985 in Victoria, Australia).

6. The word *good* is not an easy word to use in a postmodern writing culture. Dare we say *what* is 'good'? Whenever we have used 'good', in this text, we have used it in an evaluative sense and not merely a relativistic sense; context will shape the meaning used.

   Constructs such as 'fair', 'true', 'right' (and wrong!) can be derived from those natural rights and values that centre on *the right to feel safe, the right to dignity and fair treatment, the right to learn.*

When the United Nations Convention on the Rights of the Child was drawn up in 1959, the tenor of the 10 principles was that those rights are *entitlements* and (by inference of natural law) – good for the child as right for the child whether it is the right to 'protection from cruelty, neglect and exploitation' or ' free education, play and recreation'. By any definition these are good for (and to) the child. (See Rogers, 1998.)

In the 1989 Declaration, fifty-four detailed Articles define the rights of children under four categories:

1. Prevention (of illness/neglect);
2. Provision (of education with specific reference to children who are disabled);
3. Protection (from abuse and exploitation);
4. Participation (in decisions which affect them).

These categories have been widely used as a framework for educational and behaviour management practice; as we have in this book.

See also Cathy Nutbrown (2006) for a discussion on the issue of rights in education.

7. Again 'right' and 'wrong' are always used in this text with the framework of the rights of the child. We believe that certain kinds of management, discipline and punishment are wrong (or right) dependent not merely on goodwill or good intentions but based on 'rights' and 'values' we hold about the way we ought to treat children.

   We find it ludicrous that some educational writers (not practitioners) suggest we should not say to a child that such and such a behaviour is 'wrong'. While some children's backgrounds affect, and even predispose, their behaviour to hostile or aggressive expression, it is still wrong to hit someone if they will not pass a pencil; it is still wrong to spit at others or calculatingly bully them.

8. The issue of individual behaviour management plans is addressed, at length, in Chapter 6.

9. While play (free, symbolic or structured) is an essential feature of a child's development the purpose (and place) of play in early years is not the purpose, or scope, of this book. We are well aware (from our experience and our reading) that symbolic play enables both cognitive and social competencies, professional perspective-taking and co-operation. Some children – sadly – have had little experience of symbolic play prior to pre-school and primary school. There is substantial research detailing the positive benefits of play (including play therapy) but we have left this topic to others and kept our focus on the overriding purpose of this book – early years and behaviour management.

10. Obviously this is different (and naturally more demanding) as a subject teacher (art, music, language …).

11. While it is clear that there is wide variability, and tolerance, of noise volume in a classroom, it is also clear that no one classroom is a law unto itself. If the noise level (volume) of any given class is significantly (and frequently) affecting classes next door it is important that senior colleagues work sensitively to address that teacher's management of their class. This is not an easy matter; it is – however – a necessary professional responsibility for the good of all.

12. As noted earlier, 'subject teachers' are those teachers who take year classes for a specific subject, i.e., languages (Indonesian, Italian, French); Art; Music; Computers … Subject teachers take all children (year by year) normally for one period a week. Their role, therefore, has its own unique challenges and demands ( made easier by year teachers working with subject colleagues in the establishment phase).

13. In Australian classrooms early years teachers eat their lunches with their children most often *in the classroom.* Sometimes we go outside (in the shade) and eat our lunch there – together – as a class group. Unlike English schools, we do not have prepared hot lunches, or lunchroom areas where the whole school population sit and eat with their teachers. Also we do not have lunchtime supervisors ('dinner ladies'). *All* lunchtime supervision (as in all non-classroom supervision) is conducted by teachers.

14. Letterland is a literacy programme that has wider currency in the UK than in Australia. Each letter has its own – named – character.

15. See note 9.

16. Particularly with children diagnosed with hyperactive attention deficit behaviour and children diagnosed with autistic spectrum disorder.

17. See the website www.peersupport.edu.au. See, also, the excellent work on 'Better Buddies' by the Alannah and Madeline Foundation at www.amf.org.au.

18. In the moral development of children at early years it is not uncommon for children to see their behaviour relative to the 'superior' power of the adult to 'control' and 'punish'. This is not inconsistent with a child's egocentric view of the world and their emerging perspective-taking of others' needs and feelings. Our role, as teacher-leaders, is to enable and facilitate that growth in understanding from natural ego-centrism to *social* awareness and co-operation.

    Piaget (1932) and later Kohlberg (1971) demonstrated that children's moral development is 'stage-related' but it can be significantly aided – positively strengthened – by the quality – and nature – of adult support. Enabling children to be aware of and consider shared feelings and expectations (over merely individual interests) is one of the major challenges of Early Years education.

19. See note 12.

20. As – say – when a class seems to have become progressively unfocused, more difficult to manage; or where the teacher feels the class is more difficult to manage, to lead, to engage. In such cases colleague support is essential to discuss and plan (together) a 'fresh-start' with the class. With collegial mentoring teachers find they can often re-engage the necessary goodwill (with their children) and re-establish those rights and responsibilities. (See Rogers, 2006b.)

21. In Australia the 'Housing Commission' has (in years past) built those towering blocks of flats seen in many UK cities. Cramped, often poorly serviced and housing people whose life circumstances are often bruised, damaged, struggling and impoverished (not all impoverishment – of course – is related to economic conditions).

22. Principal – in UK terms – equates with head teacher. In Australia, head teacher equates with a senior teacher (not necessarily a principal).

23. Most bullying – at early years – occurs in playground settings. (See Rogers, 2003a.)

24. There is a very interesting study published by the *British Journal of Psychiatry* (Gresch et al., 2002) that sought to measure the effect of supplementary vitamins, minerals and essential fatty acids on the anti-social behaviour of young adult prisoners. The link between diet and anti-social behaviour is naturally difficult to measure. In this major study (funded by the Home Office in Britain) 230 young adult prisoners (in the experimental group) were given Omega 3 (and 6) along with vitamins and minerals (the control group was given a placebo). After the three-month trial, there was a statistically measurable difference recorded in anti-social behaviour (including violence) in the experimental group. This – at least – suggests there is a complex, but clear, correlative link between diet and behaviour.

In a major article in the *Guardian* newspaper several university studies researching Food Additives and Behaviour indicate a link between food additives and behaviour. Of particular note was a study conducted by Southampton University researching the link between artificial additives (particularly in soft drinks). These studies alerted the Food Standards Authority UK to release public health advice and food (and drink) additives. This raises – yet again – the critical implications for school meals/dietary policy *and* what school canteens should be selling to our children (*Guardian*, August 2007: 5–8).

There are a number of research studies addressing links between diet, nutrition and behaviour. *Classroom Magazine* (Scholastic Australia) has published a number of articles on research in this area. Of interest is the website www.adha.com.au .

25. While it seems natural, even obvious, that a child's difficult, traumatic upbringing will probably affect his behaviour and early life options in an adverse way, this should not deter us from the knowledge that non-parental environments (like school) can have a significant, and positive, moderating and mediating effect on a child's behaviour.

In a major research study by H. Rudolph Schaffer (University of Strathclyde, Glasgow, UK), "the potential of children to recover from early environmental stresses of even a quite severe and lasting nature has been underestimated in the past and that a self-righting tendency analogous to that found in physical growth can, under certain circumstances at least, be seen in psychological development too" (2000: 8).

As countless Australian teachers who have worked with traumatised migrant children will testify, school (as a social-relational environment) can provide a safe, nurturant, place and 'emotional space' not merely for formal learnings but for personal and psychological growth. See particularly the essays of D'Angelo (2004) in Rogers (ed) *How To Manage Children's Challenging Behaviour* (Sage Publications, London).

See also the seminal work by Rutter et al. (1979); Howell (1993); and Rogers (2003a). All these writers note that school is not a substitute for familial support; a school is a local learning community that enables a regular and stable environment where new learnings, understandings, hopes, choices and pathways can take place. It is within this conceptual understanding and belief that programmes like Behaviour Recovery have been developed and utilised (Rogers, 2003a).

26. One of my colleagues notes in developing a behaviour recovery plan with a young boy with Downs syndrome that she would visually cue with the 'reminder card' – briefly – when he was disruptive on the mat. This was replaced with Makaton cues (sign language). She notes, "The non-verbal instruction (and reminder cues) allowed the learning time for the whole class not to be interrupted." She further notes, "The overall result of this programme was that Matt's behaviour improved rapidly, as did the behaviour of the rest of the class (this was an unintentional bonus!)" (Rogers, 2004: 43).

27. Many of the children that we – and our colleagues – work with receive counselling support (psychologists and, sometimes, psychiatrists); some children take medication as part of their therapy. This support is, of course, crucial. It is important to remember, however, the child is still normally spending up to a third of their day *at school*.

Behaviour recovery is an *educational model* that works with other support interventions. For example, while Ritalin and Dexamphetamine (common medications prescribed for ADHD) can often assist a child's ability to concentrate, focus and attend, the child will still need to learn *how to utilise* that increased ability; this is where the individual behaviour support plans are essential.

28. Many school authorities now require a due police check process before the care-giver can work with children in the school.
29. Many primary schools include early years children in children's council meetings.
30. In a recent – and disturbing – newspaper article titled, "Parent rage (is) pushing teachers to the edge ..." the Victorian Principals' Association is quoted as saying that, "the number of incidents of parents physically and verbally abusing principals had never been higher." Quoting the Education Department of Victoria, "We have road rage, parking rage, queuing rage ... and now parent rage. It's a sign of the times. Parents have a shorter fuse ..." (*The Age Newspaper*, 10 June 2007).

    Without listing the litany of angry and aggressive behaviours (including *some* parents turning up drunk or clearly on drugs) it should be noted that it is *almost always a small group* of hostile, threatening or aggressive parents in any local community who behave in these ways. The article pointed out – however – that while the number of incidents, *overall*, is relatively low they are "increasing at a significant rate".

    The issue has largely gone unreported (publicly) "because schools were reluctant to make it known their school was having problems ... (and) for the fear of putting people off enrolling their children in (the) school ...".
31. You will note the month as February. In Australia schools begin the school year in February and end the school year in December. In the UK the school year begins in September and ends in July (like us, you follow the weather).

# Appendix A

A typical example covering letter: this parent/carer letter would accompany a primary *classroom behaviour agreement* (Chapter 3). This letter is signed by the class teacher and countersigned by the school headteacher.

*To all our parents/carers in year ...*
This behaviour agreement (plan) is for all the children, and their teacher, in Room ...

We have, with your children, discussed the issue of behaviour and learning in our first week of term one.

We discussed *what it means*:

■ *To have a class where everyone can learn well*; to the best of their ability, in ways that support each other here. We discussed issues such as: seating arrangements and groupings; reasonable noise levels; how to get teacher assistance in learning time, how to have a 'fair-go' in classroom discussions.

■ *To have a class where everyone feels safe*. We discussed physical safety but we also discussed *feeling* safe here at school: how we speak considerately to one another; what 'put-downs' are; how people feel when they are spoken to in unkind or hurtful ways. We also had a positive discussion on manners.

■ *To have a class where we treat one another with thoughtfulness, kindness and respect*. As well as discussing the issue of manners we also discussed what respect means and how to show it to others. We also discussed crucial behaviours such as consideration and co-operation.

You will see how these issues are reflected in our positive rules and responsibilities in our **classroom behaviour agreement** accompanying this letter.

### The rules

All the rules in **our classroom behaviour agreement** are there to emphasise how we protect *the right to learn, the right to feel safe and the right to respect and fair treatment.*

Our discussion on 'rights' focused on behaviours we agree are fair, right, proper, thoughtful, considerate, responsible ... We discussed the reason and purpose for our rules and the difference fair rules make.

Rules protect rights and encourage, and highlight, responsibility. This is true of all decent and fair rules (whether on the road, at home, at school, even in board games!)

We have tried to make our classroom and school rules as positive as possible with an emphasis on personal responsibility, thoughtfulness and co-operation. These rules are also published in our classroom on large posters and are the basis of any appropriate discipline.

### Encouragement

We encourage your children in many ways regarding their effort, their contributions, their participation in their life and learning here at our school. We believe that encouragement is crucial in acknowledging, affirming and supporting a child's self-esteem and growth as a person.

### Consequences (for inappropriate and wrong behaviours).

The emphasis with behaviour consequences – at our school – is not primarily on punishment but accountability and responsibility for one's behaviour. Our whole-school policy regarding use of behaviour consequences is to help our children to see a consequence as an opportunity to learn something constructive about their behaviour.

All of our children have an opportunity to have their say concerning their behaviour; where it is appropriate, children are encouraged to work out behaviour consequences with their teacher.

We seek to make the consequences fair and related to our classroom *rights*, *rules* and *responsibilities*. We believe it is very important to *relate* the behaviour consequence to the wrong behaviour, so the child sees the 'connectedness' *between behaviour, choice and outcome.*

For example we never use 'writing of lines' (or rules) as a punishment. We do detain children (on occasion) and use writing to direct their thinking and responsibility. Questions such as 'What happened and what did *you* do?', 'What rule was broken?', 'What can you do to fix things up?', 'How can your teacher help?'

If a child has broken something they will do 'community jobs' to help pay back damage and time affected by their disruptive behaviour.

If children are involved in bullying (of any kind) we always set up mediation opportunities. We also seek, at all times, to keep the respect for the individual child intact whenever we apply a behaviour consequence.

### *Support*

We make every effort to encourage and support your children to learn to the best of their ability while they are with us. Included in their learning are the choices they make about their behaviour. We will work with individual children, and the whole class group, to encourage and support responsible choices about behaviour and learning while they are with us.

We also know that children get tired, frustrated, and sometimes they get angry; we know that there will be days when children distract, disturb or disrupt others' learning; we know that children will – sometimes – hurt others unintentionally or on purpose. We need clear, fair, consequences for such behaviours.

Teachers will always support children beyond any necessary consequences for inappropriate, unacceptable and wrong behaviour.

There will always be opportunities for children to have a personal 'right of reply' concerning issues of behaviour and learning:

- to discuss their concerns with their teacher;
- to participate in class meetings where discussions about common concerns are raised, discussed, explored and often resolved by peer consultation;
- mediation, restitution and individual behaviour plans are also ways that teachers can help and enable children who may need extra support with their behaviour choices.

We would appreciate it if you would take time to read through this *classroom behaviour agreement* with your child as developed by the teacher with the class. It reflects our school's commitment to positive learning and behaviour.

We look forward to your support this year.

Yours sincerely,

Debbie Smith
February, 2007[31]

NB This letter will be countersigned by the school principal before being sent (with the class behaviour agreement) to each family.

# Appendix B

Example of a typical classroom behaviour agreement (we have used pictures – here – rather than photographs of any particular class; for ethical reasons).

Our Classroom Behaviour Agreement
Room 17

We always look after each other.
We speak kindly to others.

Lining up for class

When the bell rings we line up on our
special line.
We make room for everyone without pushing.

We walk inside our classroom.

Our carpet area.
Sitting and learning together.

We sit relaxed on the mat.
We keep our hands and feet safe.
We put our hands up to share and ask questions.

## Class work together

We always try our best.
We help one another with our classwork.
When we are working at our tables and we use
out partner-voices (our inside voices).
We share and take turns in all class activities.

## Packing up and looking after our classroom

We put things back in the right place.
We put rubbish in the bin.
We clean our tables.

## Leaving the room

We always ask our teacher before we leave our
classroom.
We always take someone with us to
the toilet.

## Our playground

We play on the junior playground equipment.
We play safely.
Look out for your buddy.
If we have a problem we ask a teacher on
playground duty.

# Appendix C

Example of a restitutional consequence

JOB SHEET

When a child has broken something the logical (related) consequence is that it is paid for.

We believe that the child should take responsibility for their choice of action. Children pay for broken equipment by completing a job sheet to 'earn' the money to replace it.

The jobs they do are community jobs which will benefit the school and they are completed during playtimes.

David

### Job Sheet

### To pay for broken car

| | |
|---|---|
| Sharpen pencils | .20p |
| Teach people to skip | .20p |
| Sort out games boxes | .20p |
| Tidy book boxes | .20p |
| Share books with children | .20p |
| TOTAL | £1 |

With thanks to Hare St. Infant School, Harlow, UK

# Appendix D

## Behaviour understandings as preferred practices

The following key behaviour understandings are taken from a group of pre-schools in Queensland which have used the behaviour language model noted earlier in this text (Chapter 4). These understandings form the basis for a model of *school-wide* preferred practices within their schools. (See also Rogers, 2006a, b.)

> *Remember to tell children exactly what you want them to do.*
> "Put the sand in the sand pit … Thanks."

> *Avoid overtalking behavioural issues. Use clear, simple, short directions.*

> *Avoid asking children 'why' questions. Instead ask 'what', 'how' and 'when' questions.*
> What is our rule …?
> When should we …?
> How do we treat …?
> Note, too, the use of inclusive language 'we', 'our' …

> *Give children specific feedback on their behaviour.*
> That was thoughtful to …
> It was very helpful when …

> *Invite co-operation by giving conditional directions. Try to use:*
> 'Yes – when',
> 'When – then',
> 'After – then' statements.
> "Yes, we can play outside – when we have put our toys away."

> *When faced with behavioural issues remember to:*
> Remain calm.
> Give clear instruction to the child.
> Follow-up and follow-through.
> When the child complies, praise and move on.

# Bibliography

Bernard, M. and Joyce, M. (1984) *Rational-Emotive Therapy with Children and Adolescents*. New York: John Wiley and Sons.

Breheney, C., Mackrill, V. and Grady, N. (1996) *Making Peace at Mayfield: A Whole-School Approach to Behaviour Management*. Melbourne: Eleanor Curtain. NB This is one of those rare – special – books about the power of a school to make a difference; to give hope; to engender meaningful and significant change in a demanding and challenging socio-economic setting. This book is a case study of a school that made a powerful difference in their local community – who refused to allow difficult and demanding challenges from working against their beliefs about effecting change.

Clough, P., Garner, P., Pardeck, J.T. and Yuen, F. (2005) *Handbook of Emotional and Behavioural Difficulties*. London: Sage Publications.

Dempster, M. and Raff, D. (1992) *Class Discussions: A Powerful Classroom Strategy*. Melbourne: (K-12) Hawker-Brownlow Education.

Dreikurs, R. (1968) *Psychology in the Classroom: A Manual For Teachers*. New York: Harper and Row.

Dreikurs, R. Grunwald, B. and Pepper, F. (1982) *Maintaining Sanity in the Classroom*. New York: Harper and Row.

Forsey, C. (1994) *Hands Off!: The Anti-violence Guide to Developing Positive Relationships*. West Education Centre Inc. ISBN 0 9 589708 9 0.

Gillborn, D., Nixon, J. and Rudduck, J. (1992) *Dimensions of Discipline: Rethinking Practice in Secondary Schools*. London: Department for Education.

Ginott, H. (1971) *Teacher and Child*. New York: Macmillan.

Gresch, C. B., Hammon, S. M., Hampson, S. E., Eves, A. and Crowder, M. J. (2002) 'Influence of supplementary vitamins, minerals and essential fatty acids on the antisocial behaviour of young adult prisoners', *British Journal of Psychiatry*, 181: 22–8.

Hall, J. (1993) *Confident Kids: Helping Your Child Cope With Fear*. Melbourne: Lothian Press.

Howell, K. (1993) 'Eligibility and need: is there a difference in being disturbed and being disturbing?', in D. Evans, M. Myhill and J. Izard (eds), *Student Behaviour Problems: Positive Initiatives and New Frontiers*. Melbourne: ACER.

Kohlberg, L. (1971) 'Moral development', in C. M. Beck, B. S. Crittendon and E. V. Sullivan (eds), *Moral Education : Inter-disciplinary Approaches*. Toronto: University of Toronto Press.

Kohlberg, L. (1976) 'Moral stages and moralization: the cognitive-developmental approach', in T. Licona (ed), *Moral Development and Behaviour: Theory, Research and Issues*. New York: Holt Rinehart and Winston.

Lee, C. (2004) *Preventing Bullying in Schools*. London: Paul Chapman Publications.

Lindon, J. (2007) *Understanding Child Development: Linking Theory and Practice*. Abingdon: Hodder–Arnold.

Marion, M. (2000) 'Guiding young children's understanding and management of anger', *Education Horizons*, 6(3): 5–8.

McGrath H. and Francey, S. (1993) *Friendly Kids, Friendly Classrooms*. Melbourne: Longman Cheshire.

Morgan, D. P. and Jenson, W. R. (1988) *Teaching Behaviourally Disordered Children: Preferred Practices*. Toronto: Merrill Publishing Co.

Nutbrown, C. (2006) *Key Concepts in Early Childhood Education and Care*. London: Sage.

Piaget, J. (1932) *The Moral Judgement of the Child*. London: Routledge & Kegan Paul.

Rickard, J. (1994) *Relaxation For Children*. Melbourne: ACER Press.

Rigby, K. (1996) *Bullying in Schools: What to do about it*. Melbourne: Australian Council for Educational Research.

Roffey, S. and O'Reirdan, T. (1997) *Infant Classroom Behaviour: Needs Perspectives and Strategies*. London: David Fulton.

Rogers, B. (1998) *You Know the Fair Rule*. (Second edition). Melbourne: ACER.

Rogers, B. (2002) *I Get By With a Little Help: Colleague Support in Schools*. ACER Press, Melbourne. (In the U.K. published by Paul Chapman (Sage Publications), London.)

Rogers, B. (2003a) *Behaviour Recovery: A Whole School Programme for Mainstream Schools*. Camberwell, Vic.: ACER. (In the UK published by Paul Chapman (Sage Publications), London.)

Rogers, B. (2003b) *Effective Supply Teaching: Behaviour Management, Classroom Discipline and Colleague Support*. London: Paul Chapman (Sage Publications).

Rogers, B. (2004) *How to Manage Children's Challenging Behaviour*. London: Sage Publications.

Rogers, B. (2006a) *Behaviour Management: A Whole School Approach*. 2nd edn. Sydney: Scholastic. (In the UK published by Paul Chapman (Sage Publications), London.)

Rogers, B. (2006b) *Cracking the Hard Class: Strategies for Managing the Harder than Average Class*. (2nd edn). Sydney: Scholastic. (In the UK published by Paul Chapman (Sage Publications), London.)

Rutter, M. (1983) 'School effects on pupil progress: research findings and policy implications', *Child Development*, 54: 1–29.

Rutter, M,, Maughan, B., Mortimer, P. and Ousten, J. (1979) *Fifteen Thousand Hours: Secondary Schools and Their Effects on Children*. London: Open Books.

Schaffer, H. R. (2000) 'The early experience assumption: past, present and future', *International Journal of Behavioural Development*, 24(1): 5–14.

Slee, P. and Rigby, K. (1991) 'Bullying among Australian children: reported behaviour and attitude towards victims', *Journal of Social Psychology*, 131: 615–27.

Smith, P. and Thompson, D. (eds) (1991) *Practical Approaches to (Dealing with) Bullying*. London: Fulton Price.

Stephenson, P. and Smith, D. (1989) 'Bullying in the junior school', in D. P. Tattum and D. A. Lane (eds), *Bullying in Schools*. Stoke-on-Trent: Trentham Books.

Stones, R. (1992) *No More Bullying!* London: Dinosaur Publications, HarperCollins.

Tulloch, R. and Greeder, A. (1990) *Danny in the Toybox*. (A Scholastic picture-story book addressing childhood anger.) Sydney: Scholastic Books.

Wheldhall, K. (1992) *Discipline in Schools. Psychological Perspectives on the Elton Report*. London: Routledge.

Whitbread, D. (ed) (2000) *The Psychology Of Teacher and Learning In the Primary School*. London: RoutledgeFarmer.

White, P. (1961) *Riders in the Chariot*. London: Penguin.

# Important websites

Carer Support and Schools: www.sofweb.vic.edu.au
The Children, Youth and Family Act 2005 (became law in April, 2007 is the legislative base for current reforms to child protection and family services). See www.office-for-children.vic.gov.au/ece
A helpful web address for attention deficit spectrum disorder: www.bigpond.com/addiss
   Some websites that address bullying:

www.education.unisa.edu.au/bullying
www.antibullying.net
www.bullystoppers.com
www.kidscape.org.uk
www.dfes.gov.uk/bullying
www.bbc.co.uk/schools/bullying

The Nurture Group Network: www.nurture_groups.org

# Index

Accountability meeting 107, 108

Aggression 104, 127–130

Anger (in children) 92, 126–131 (*see also* frustration tolerance)

Angry parents 140–142, 147 (fn. 30)

Anger (in teachers) 75, 85, 89

Autism (Asperger's syndrome) 7, 11, 29

Argumentative behaviour in children 50, 61–65

Arguing and squabbling (among children) 67–69

Assertion 14, 71–72 (*see also* Desists)

Assistance by teacher (during on-task learning time) 27–29

Attention to children (during whole-class teaching time) 9, 11–19

Attentional behaviour 111–113, 117, 121, 124

Attention Deficit Spectrum Behaviour 111

Bad-day syndrome 6

Bad language (*see* swearing)

Behaviour awareness (in children) 51, 54, 55, 61, 85, 118, 119, 121, 126 (*see also* responsibilities)

Behaviour ownership 61, 89, 126 (*see also* consequences)

Behaviour plans (individual behaviour plans for children) 113–120

Behaviour Recovery 113–114, 123, 146 (Fn. 27)

Blocking ('verbal blocking' as a corrective cue) 64, 65

Boundaries (*see* roles and responsibilities)

Bullying 105–106, 108, 151

Calling-out behaviour 17, 54, 63, 115

Calming (of class group) 3
    communicating calmness 13–14, 68, 72

Causitive pathology 109–110, 146 (fn. 25)

Carpet time 11–12, 23, 35, 115

'Carers' (*see* parent/carers)

Choices (in behaviour management and discipline contexts) 50, 51, 57, 58, 69, 73, 84, 151

Classroom Behaviour Agreements (whole-class) 37–44 (*see also* Appendix A and B)

Classroom meetings 41, 151
    classroom meeting to address bullying 106

Colleague support x, 31, 44, 111, 114, 124

Cool-off time (*see* time-out)

Consequences (behaviour consequences for inappropriate, unacceptable, wrong or dangerous behaviour) 42, 46, 47, 83–91, 150

'certainty principle' 51, 74, 84, 89, 100